T0164582

THRIVIN'

THE AMERICAN DREAM

*A Story of Unwavering
Determination, Adversity
Too Heavy to Withstand,
and a Sheer Grit to Win*

Jason Camper
with Don Yaeger

ENVISION BOOKS

Copyright © 2021 by Jason Camper

No part of this publication may be reproduced, stored in a retrieval system, or transmitted in any form by any means, electronic, mechanical, photocopying, or otherwise, without the prior written permission of the publisher.

This book is available in quantity at special discounts for your group or organization. For further information, contact:

Envision Books
An imprint of Triumph Books LLC
814 North Franklin Street
Chicago, Illinois 60610
(312) 337-0747
www.triumphbooks.com

ISBN: 978-1-62937-972-2
Printed in U.S.A.
Design by Patricia Frey

Contents

Introduction

When the conversations with my co-author began, one of the first big moments came when he asked me to explain exactly why writing this book was important to me. I shared, simply, that I've always found inspiration in learning the journey that people like me have taken on their path to success. And because I see myself as "just a guy," I believe my journey will connect with many. As you'll read, I came from humble upbringings in West Texas. And I will never forget where it all started. I wasn't a product of a fancy education…in fact, I never graduated college. So if there's any way that what has happened to me, the life lessons that I've gone through, can impact others, I gladly want to share it.

I speak to audiences often and am asked my opinion on success. My answer: I feel like a lot of people are trying to find the shortcut to success. Many have been looking for the shortcut for success since the beginning of time. It's simply not there. Or, if it is there, it didn't show up for me. Success is about grit, it's about a lot of hard work, a lot of determination. I often find people have a lackadaisical approach to what they're trying to accomplish in life. My journey may speak to a lot of things, but it speaks mostly to "want." I wanted it. Bad. The amount of time it took me to get where I was trying to get, those hardships that come from that effort…just know it's possible. And yours doesn't have to take as long as my journey took. But there's a price to be paid. Still, it is possible. The end result, the outcome you're looking to accomplish in your life, whatever your goals, whatever your mission is, it is possible.

I've always loved the underdog movies. *Cinderella Man* is a great one. You're looking at a guy who didn't make it in the boxing world, his family's destitute, broke, and they're not going to eat unless he provides. That's when people want it badly. That's when the willpower increases and big things happen. You see a person's perseverance really kick in. Until you are able to find that emotional horsepower within you for what's important to you, what's important to your life, this pursuit becomes even more difficult. But once the horsepower kicks in, the future is bright.

One more thing I wanted to do with this book: encourage people to pick a course and stay with it. Fail, get back up and fight forward. Don't turn left or right when it gets tough. Stay on the path. You get paid for what you know, not for what you do. And that knowledge is what enables you to win. In this book I share with you my many disappointments. Many people saw them as failures. I saw them as monumental learning moments. So I encourage you to learn from your moments when things don't go well. Get up and keep charging.

That's how you THRIVE!

CHAPTER 1

Steppingstones

There I was, at the tallest point in Cabo San Lucas, perched so high above the mountain that the curvature of the Sea of Cortez began to melt into the darkening sky off into the distance. As I watched the sun slowly set on this majestic scene from my pool deck, I breathed in the fresh air and scanned the landscape. How had I gotten here? For the first time in my life, it began to hit me. Below, along the foundation of the house, I saw this pathway of steppingstones leading down the side of the mountain. My mind raced through flashbacks of my life—from the plains of West Texas to my time in Nashville to building a company worth hundreds of millions of dollars in Dallas, Texas—and it began to feel so intentional, almost like destiny. All these moments in my life that I had once thought were failures, opportunities that hadn't amounted to anything, I now saw as part of my journey to success. I could picture myself jumping from one steppingstone to the next. Instead of giving up when I slipped, I moved on to the next stone. Every time one didn't work, I had a choice. I could turn and go back, or I could look ahead for the next steppingstone. Each was a life lesson that enabled the steps forward. Finally, I could see the meaning for all those hurdles in life. Those moments of adversity were my personal steppingstones. Each step led to the top of this mountain.

My revelation from this altitude came in the middle of Le-Vel's explosion. The company I had founded in 2012 was now like a rocket with afterburners firing off and propelling us. At the start, it was me, my business partner Paul Gravette and our Director of Technology Justin Rouleau. Paul was in charge of sales, Justin was running IT and I was running the show. By "show." I mean supply chain, legal, compliance, marketing, customer service, finance, accounting, logistics and fulfillment. It was my job to make sure Le-Vel manufactured unique, game-changing products, processed and fulfilled orders on time, paid commissions on schedule, and had proper customer support—everything that included operating the company and keeping the train on the tracks. In Year 1 we had done $10 million in sales. That was followed by $100 million in Year 2, $250 million in Year 3 and $350 million in Year 4. Can you imagine? We were growing by hundreds of millions of dollars a year. We had all these products to manage and all these people to look out for and I was insanely focused on shipping product on time, avoiding backorders and paying our vendors and protecting Le-Vel's good name and Thrive brand so that no one ever had a bad word to say. I was in the thick of everything exploding at Le-Vel and had never really stopped to take it all in. Now, I stood looking out at the calm water below, and I finally stopped to look at the stones and the path. It was as if I was seeing those steppingstones for the very first time and realized I would never have been able to do what I was doing for Le-Vel had I not gone through the dark times I went through to make my way along the path.

Most people in life are directionless. The reality is, many of us have spent large portions of our life in what feels like a pinball machine, pinging from one side to the other and back again. One thing doesn't work and—Boom!—we try something else. My journey was defined by persistence. Ultimately, I ended up on this path of steppingstones that defined my life. In their own way, each one took me to where I am today as the leader of a multi-billion-dollar company. I had to experience these hurdles; had to suffer through them.

I didn't view these moments as steppingstones when they happened. I never thought to myself, "Oh my God, I just fell on my face, but look what I learned!" We don't go through life knowing what these lessons are. But where I'm at in life now, I can look backward and see with clearer eyes. Early on in my life, though, as I struggled with business, left jobs because I wasn't successful or watched companies I worked for collapse, I didn't view it that way. My first job in the industry of direct selling, at a company called AdvoCare, was a colossal financial failure. I thought that AdvoCare was all for nothing. And when I moved to a company called Burn Lounge later and felt like I had it all figured out, the world collapsed overnight when the company was shut down by regulators. I certainly didn't see any silver lining then. Now I see those phases in my life as steppingstones I can point to and say, "Here's what this did for me." Each stone in my life may not have been successful, but it led me to something greater. So many people think the direct selling industry doesn't work, but that is how I earned more than $400 million (at the time this book was written), met my wife and built a multi-billion-dollar business. Direct sales worked for me—but only because I went through so many periods in my life where I had to keep going if I wanted to make it happen. I often tell people my journey was about "failing forward." Keep in mind, my journey and my failing forward happen to be in the direct sales industry. However, what I've learned in life and what I write about in this book applies to all industries alike.

The No. 1 pitfall I see with unsuccessful people is they're just not determined enough, they don't have thick skin, they give up too easily, they throw in the towel. So many people in this world are unwilling to do what the five percent are to be successful. You have to be willing to be scarred and bruised by failure to truly thrive in the end. My dad likes to joke today that the traits which made me so difficult to deal with when I was younger became the same ones that led to where I am now. My unwillingness to take "no" for an answer got me into so much trouble as a teen. Nobody could ever tell me "no," nobody could ever tell me what to do, nobody could ever tell me "stop." But that same persistence and having thick skin helped me later on in life and ultimately in business.

Wherever you are now as you're reading this, whatever industry you're in, whatever you're going through, it's a steppingstone to your ultimate destination. It's OK to fail forward. I feel I'm talented and sharp, but I don't feel like I'm some supreme being. The Good Book says, "Keep on knocking, and the door will be opened to you." I tell my team all the time, "Does it say knock for 10 days and if you don't get what you want, walk away and quit?" No! The people that truly get what they want out of life are the people that don't give up. I know you've heard that before, but how many of us live it?

Everybody loves the underdog story because the underdog story is generally true. I wasn't super educated. I wasn't from a family that had a lot of money. There was nothing about me at a young age that you would point to and say, "This guy is going to be unbelievably successful." Nobody could see it. I found out through this journey and through my many steppingstones what I was made of.

You can go do something special in life. It's not just these "special people" out there. If you're willing to put in the work, if you're willing to make sound decisions in your life, you can climb mountains. I always knew in my heart that I had what it took to become successful, even when I had little to build that vision around. I didn't know how to get there or what to do, but I believed I had the skillset. It wasn't like I woke up every day thinking I was going to be successful. I didn't have certainty in the future. When you go through dark adversity, that spirit of, "I can do this," does diminish. But I always believed I had what it took to become successful. I was trying like many of us in life, to find the path to get there. Winning is about dreaming, working for what you want in life and pressing on. What are your goals? What dreams are you willing to jump steppingstones to achieve no matter how bloody you get or how tired you become? Will you keep jumping forward? Will you keep failing onward?

So many people give up on what they're seeking before they can really build any momentum. Maybe you know that struggling realtor who gave up after a few years and said, "Well, this isn't working." They went to work in a gym before they decided maybe they should be an insurance agent instead. People jump around so much they never give themselves the chance to truly take off. It took a lot of steppingstones for me to get where I am today, but I didn't quit. I was forced to make decisions of where to jump next, but I stayed on the same path. There was a point in my life where I tried to quit. Thank the Lord I didn't and persevered on. There are no shortcuts in life. You have to keep going and do your best to avoid the sharp or slippery steps along the way.

The journey will never be picture perfect, that's a guarantee. Today I'm very grateful for homes all over the world, a private jet and I have more cars than underwear, but it certainly wasn't always that way. I want to make sure you read that sentence correctly though: I don't have those things because I got lucky or because someone willed them to me. I earned everything I have, and I have plenty of scars to show for it. I remember my darkest, most depressing moment as I tried to make my journey in direct selling work. "What do I have to freaking do?" I said to my wife while sitting on the staircase of the house we were renting at the time in Irving. I passionately pleaded with her, "Babe, this industry works! It does! I just need one of these to go. We just need one." The conversation had reached this point because my wife had suggested maybe I try something else. "Look what you've gone through, look what keeps happening. Maybe it's time to do something else," she said. But I knew it could work. If everything could just align properly and if I could find the right place for the talents I was bringing, I believed I could hit a home run. I saw this industry work firsthand in a very, very meaningful way when I dropped out of college to pursue this journey. Getting dragged through the minefield of direct sales only made me stronger. I knew it could happen and was unwilling to quit simply because of the bad results and mistakes along the way. Sure, I made mistakes and will own those. But it wasn't just me. I'd come up with reasons to keep pressing on in this world despite failures. I would tell myself, "This could have been really good, but this roadblock was here and it was beyond your control." I always had that vision of going forward, making it better the next time and not suffering from the same pitfalls.

Looking back now, there were no "missteps" along the way, although they all seemed like missteps at the time. Every one of those moments, it turned out, was a step I had to take. I didn't know then how many more steps there were, but I knew when I hit solid ground it was going to be very fulfilling. I kept looking ahead to the next steppingstone, a willpower to keep stepping forward. The truth of success is you have to keep looking for the steppingstone. Most people stop way too early.

My story is one of a teenager whose photo today could have a Texas Department of Corrections number underneath his name. It is also one of a young man who could have given up on business and my personal dream of succeeding in direct sales when one failure followed another. As I stood overlooking the ocean that evening and stared at the stones, I finally saw how the many stories and choices had defined my journey. What if I had turned back when I failed? Where would I be standing now had I stopped leaping forward in search of achieving my dreams?

By God's grace, and by a desire to define success somewhere in life, that young man happened into an industry and began chasing a dream that has changed his life and the lives of millions.

This is that story.

CHAPTER 2

Early Wake-Up Call

t was just after 3 a.m. on a late spring Sunday as my dad led me out of the Lubbock, Texas, jailhouse and across the brick pavers on Main Street to the Lubbock Bail Bond building for the fourth consecutive weekend. Like déjà vu, my dad paid the bail bondsman and we quietly walked to my parents' maroon Dodge minivan parked outside.

For several years I had absolutely tortured my parents with my unruly behavior, and it hit an apex during my senior year of high school. I was getting arrested left and right and there was nothing anybody could say or do that would stop me and my behavior. I was the leader of the limelight, or so it felt, of our big group of high school friends, and we partied non-stop. We were out of control. During my final month of high school, it was like clockwork. I'd get arrested in the early hours of Sunday morning after partying all night Saturday, I'd call my dad, he'd bail me out and I'd promise it wouldn't happen again. This went on for three consecutive weekends—for driving while intoxicated, public intoxication and evading arrest—before my dad delivered a stern warning. "Jason, we've done everything we can," he told me in his even-keeled tone. "Your mother and I can't keep spending this money and we can't keep doing this. If you get arrested again, don't call, because I'm not coming to get you. I need you to understand how serious I am." I told him as I always did that it wouldn't happen again. Really, I just didn't plan on getting caught.

But my promise, like most of my life at that time, wasn't genuine. The next Saturday night, after I had partied again, I was drunkenly driving home in my Chevy T-Top Camaro when flashing red and blue lights hit my rearview mirror. I was two blocks from home, but for the fourth-straight weekend I was headed downtown to the jailhouse. At 18 years old it wasn't like I had a long list of phone numbers to call. So, with no other options, I dialed home once again. To my surprise, my dad showed up to the jailhouse and then again wrote a check to get me out.

This time though, something different happened, something I can't explain. But it changed my life. As I sat in the passenger seat of the parked van, my mind hit hyperdrive. Everything began racing through my head. All the instances of me getting in trouble, all the arrests, all the court hearings, all the images of my parents striking checks to bail me out. I remembered the way my dad had looked at me just the week before, the way he had told me he wasn't coming to bail me out again. I had believed him, and yet there he was in the driver's seat, ready to take me home. Why? Why didn't he give up on me? Why was there so much unconditional love? For years I had been a tough guy willing to take on anybody with no signs of softness or emotion, just a sheer, wannabe badass. But in that moment, I completely cracked. I began crying uncontrollably. The person I was, at that moment, completely shattered. The real Jason Camper was about to emerge.

I didn't have any idea why I shattered that night. But I do now. That unconditional love broke everything. It triggered the rush of memories or the wave of guilt and emotions. There were tears and there was remorse. My head and heart had been so hardened, almost as if there was a shell casing around them. I didn't listen to anybody. Nobody could tell me anything. I had all the answers and everything else was bullshit. Nothing could get to me.

And then suddenly the power of love from and for my family broke through. Whether it was divine intervention, whether it was how my parents had handled the situation, whether it was a combination of those and other pressure points, it all finally broke me. "Jason, what are you doing to your family?" I thought to myself as I sat in the parked van, tears streaming down my face. The person I had been pretending to be and had been acting as was suddenly gone. The next day, after laying in my room thinking about everything, I went to the living room and sat next to my dad on the couch. "Dad," I said. "I don't want to stand out anymore." It was one of the most important things I've ever said. My parents had this unwillingness to give up on me. Now, I was determined to turn it all around.

AT AN EARLY AGE I felt like I could achieve something different than a stereotypical 9-5 job like I had watched my father work. I didn't have a sour taste in my mouth about my dad's work. I just imagined other ways to make a great living had to be out there. My childhood and early years were filled with structure. I was brought up from the cotton fields of West

Texas with my cousins. I had a very conservative, Christian upbringing filled with dos and don'ts. On Sunday mornings we were up bright and early and got to South Plains Church of Christ on time without fail. I was a difficult child, and I remember every Sunday morning, instead of trying to get me out of bed 15 times in a row, my dad would put canned cinnamon rolls in the oven (he knew my favorite food would do the trick). I'd smell them and race into the kitchen. We'd go home after morning service, eat lunch and get ready for Sunday night service. On Wednesday we'd do it again. I couldn't watch PG-rated movies. Everything was, "No, no, no, no, no, no."

Looking back, I cherish my background and upbringing, but I was required to walk a very tight rope. My mom's family was full of hunters, welders and farmers. My dad's family was a mixed background of members who served in the Air Force and the Army. My mom made $19,000 a year working at Lubbock Christian University, and my dad made $80,000 a year as an air traffic controller. My father lived by an "as-needed" philosophy. Already have one pair of shoes? What do you need two for? We purchased clothes one time a year before school started. I'm not complaining. We had food on the table and a roof over our head.

Through my teenage years, as a person that's very driven, I wanted to own a lot of things I thought of as cool (go-karts, dirt bikes, fancy bicycles). But given dad's feelings that I didn't "need" those things, I had to pay for those things myself. When I was 11 years old I really wanted a little dog and knew a lady who had a Dachshund. That Fourth of July, I went back and forth with her, bartering on the price until we finally reached an agreement. It might have been the first time I had wheeled and dealed to get what I wanted. We named him Rocket Red Glare for the occasion. My upbringing fostered a persistent drive like no other, a drive that grew as I got older. If I had been brought up and given everything, I don't think I would have the drive that I have today. I don't know if someone could have more drive, more motivation, more determination to go get what they wanted than what I developed.

I didn't know how to go get the things I desired, I didn't know how to go win, I didn't know how other people were doing and getting these things. All I knew was that I didn't want a status quo life. I always felt early on that something was different with me, for me, about me.

That was put in my mind during elementary school. I never wanted to sit still. I was athletic, and all I wanted to do was go play. Teachers thought I had a severe learning disability. That turned into doctors, which turned into medication, which turned into "what's wrong with him?" Truth is, nothing was wrong with me. I was just never stimulated in school. I was so bored that I frankly was never really very good at it. Around sixth grade, I began getting into fights. There was a lot of uncontrollable, rebellious activity, which turned into my parents scratching their heads, with no idea what to do. They fought the notion that I had a learning disability, so they pulled me out of public schools and began homeschooling me. The problem was, I had already been introduced to this public party—school, kids, fun—and here I was at 12 years old, starting to mature socially, and I was stuck at home. It was torture for me getting home-schooled. I'd get so mad at my parents for making me do my schoolwork and fought them until the bitter end about it. The only thing that ever motivated me was competition. When my dad would teach me Algebra or Geometry, he'd challenge me to a race to solve the problem. The bragging rights and satisfaction locked me in. I got home-schooled for seventh and eighth grade and pleaded constantly with my parents to let me go back. Tired of listening to me, they finally broke down and sent me back to school for ninth grade. But once I got released back into the public school system, I went absolute ballistic.

During my two years of homeschooling I met my first best friend, Greg Bernstein, through a competitive soccer league. Greg's parents were night and day different from mine. His parents let him do whatever he wanted to do. They had a different definition of raising children. My parents thought along the lines of, "We're going to tell you exactly what to do and you're going to do it." His parents gave him freedom and free rein and expected Greg to follow the rules in return. I loved hanging out at Greg's house because we could be and do whatever we wanted.

So when Greg and I got together, we hit another level. My friendship with Greg was great, but that window included our introduction to drugs. We began experimenting with marijuana, mushrooms, ecstasy and whatever else we could get our hands on. I was arrested for possession of marijuana in ninth grade. Not long after, while on probation, I got into a fight at a pool hall, which led to me spending 45 days in juvenile detention going into 10th grade. I remember the little bay window in the juvenile detention cell. It was frosted glass, so you could see light but you couldn't see any details. It was very much self isolation. I was an inmate. I had a come-to-Jesus moment during those 45 days. I remember thinking how bad I wanted to be out of there and how bad I wanted to go home and have my mom's meals. I even wanted to go to church and have that routine back. It seemed like the greatest thing. I remember reading *The Barrio Kings*, about a boy who gave up gang life after his brother was killed in a street fight. I felt empowered and motivated. Let me out, I promised, and I'll be a different kid.

When I finally got out of juvie, I let go of the drugs. By that time, Greg and I began separating. He was a year behind me, still in junior high, and I was now in high school. I was playing football and seemed to be doing better. But that come-to-Jesus moment only lasted for 30 days or so. Then it started fading.

In high school I met my second best friend, Jarod Roach. That's when my phase with partying and alcohol and girls went into hyperdrive. We had a big, tight-knit party group. I was a natural born leader, I guess, and it wasn't a good time for me to begin to show it. But I did. I got in more trouble than everybody else because I was willing to go the farthest and do the most audacious things. I loved being the life of the party, making jokes and proving I could push the envelope. Partying and drugs weren't anything my parents lived or understood, so they didn't know how to handle me. Detention still didn't tame me. Nothing really rocked me. Looking back, that was my biggest problem. I thought every rule or law was a suggestion. I wanted to go do my thing, and doing my thing oftentimes wasn't the most beneficial. The summers were when things really took off. Jarod and I worked together as lifeguards, so we had a little spending money and free time. We had a lot in common. We both loved working out, chasing girls, and having a blast. That's when the arrests started racking up.

My parents did everything they could to rein me in. My dad took the door off my bedroom and nailed my windows shut. Instead, I started quietly tiptoeing out the front door. One time, I left the garage door open two feet and slid underneath it later that night. I was determined to get what I wanted. Every time I would get in trouble, it was always the same routine. My dad would show disappointment, but never anger. My mom, on the other hand, was not afraid to show she was extremely mad. She would come out of the bedroom to talk to me when we got home from the jailhouse. Every time I would get out of jail my dad would try to get me to talk. He was destroyed. "Dad, I know. I know," I'd tell him. "It's not going to happen again." Like clockwork, there would be an early-morning Sunday call from the jailhouse the next week. "OK, let me talk to your mother," he'd say. He told me he could never go to sleep because he always knew the phone was going to ring. At one point, he unplugged the phone before plugging it back in because that didn't ease the pain, either. They always knew the phone call was going to come. I watched my dad stroke all these $1,500 or $2,000 checks to a lawyer for all my legal troubles.

My dad tried to teach me lessons, but they seldom fazed me. One time he came to bail me out and they told him it'd be $25. "What happens if I don't pay the $25?" he asked. "He gets to spend another night in jail," they told him. I watched as he turned around and walked out, leaving me to spend one more night behind bars.

I was likely on the radar of the Lubbock Police by my fourth arrest of that month my senior year. I had bleached hair back then. I can only imagine a West Texas conservative-type police officer pulling me over and seeing a punk-looking kid in a sleeveless shirt with bleached hair and piercings. And if they weren't judging by appearances, they'd still get my driver's license, go back to their police car and see my war tab of mischief and destruction. Still, I felt invincible. I was going to find a way not to get caught.

We don't ever know how or why in life things land as they do. There are so many scenarios where things could have gone even worse for me, or I could have gotten killed, or more tragically, hurt someone else. I could have continued on with my hellion behavior. Had I made it those final two blocks home that night, where might my life have gone? Would I have ever cracked? Would it have been too late? I believed my dad when he said he wasn't going to bail me out of jail for a fourth time. Yet I still called, and he still came. What if he hadn't?

As my cases brewed in the legal system, I remember my dad's attorney telling me that the District Attorney wanted to push for 2-4 years in prison. It wasn't the threat from the lawyer that broke me. I'd been hearing those warnings for four years by then, from my parents and teachers and youth minister. None of that stuff mattered to me. It was truly the power of love that my parents showed that finally cracked the barrier around my heart. When the legal battles finally came to an end,

I was given a deferred adjudication and five years of felony probation with monthly drug testing. I was in an astronomical amount of trouble. I completely went off the radar of all those friends I had partied with previously. I was actually OK with it. I was happy going to church again and became more open to trying to talk to people at church instead of thinking everybody there was a dork and that I didn't have anything in common with any of them. I was very much into "learning" how to be a good person, being a person that my dad always used to tell me that I needed to be, to fit in society. I was finally on that path.

I was heading toward a very long-term, destructive life up to that last arrest. The sheer power of love is what, at that moment, shattered my life, in a good way. I started to repair my life and stopped being a destructive, hard-hearted person. I became more accepting. I started establishing a relationship with the Lord. There was a feeling of someone looking out for me as I began reflecting. For whatever reason, my life wasn't supposed to go deeper into the judicial system, that was not my destiny. There was almost a supernatural feeling of somebody guiding me and saying, "Hey, head over here, not over there."

I was so determined to do something great with my life but faced a constant battle of self-worth for the next five years. My probation officer would constantly demean me and bring me down. He would even look at me in a very perverted way while he watched me urinate for my monthly drug test. I could see how people would get in trouble and never change. It was almost like the system was designed for people to never really get out unless they were truly determined to change their life. No matter how good things were going, my probation officer would tell me I was never going to amount to anything, that I was always going to be a reject. I was trying to reshape my identity, but the probation system was adamantly telling me I was going to mess it all up and that no matter what happened, deep down, I was never going to change. I remember the exit interview with the head of the department after I had completed my five-year probation period. She told me my life was essentially ruined because of what I'd done and that there was essentially no chance of me turning my life around. But that wasn't a decision she got to make. We all go through tough times, but we still have the chance to burst through and persevere. That's life. You get a curveball and have to pick yourself back up, get through it, and learn from it. It's not about a participation ribbon. It's about do you want to win or not? I was determined to win, and that meant proving those people wrong. Don't talk about it. Be about it.

I don't know what might have happened had I not gotten arrested that fourth time or if my dad didn't come bail me out that night. Every day there are moments of fate that help define our journey in life, the direction we go. You sometimes wonder who is looking out for you. I call myself a Christian. I say my prayers. I'm not a perfect person, but I can definitely say there has been a higher presence looking out for me in life, whether that means guiding me in certain ways or guiding my parents to not give up. From the moment my life cracked that night in my parent's minivan in front of the bail bondsman, I've never even had a speeding ticket. That was THE turning point in my life.

CHAPTER 3

Friday Night Lights (and Partying)

n January of my senior year of high school I remember standing on the indoor soccer field and surveying the crowd for my parents. I looked up and down the bleachers, side-to-side, scanning for their faces. "Huh," I thought as a pit hit my stomach. For the first time in my athletic career, my mom and dad were nowhere to be seen.

It wasn't uncommon for me to be hanging out with a soccer friend and then catch a ride to the game. But I always enjoyed looking up into the stands to see my parents when I was playing. Even in the younger years before I was driving, while some parents dropped their kids off to practice or games and then left, my parents were at everything. My mom and dad came to every game, every practice. And if one couldn't make it, the other always would.

While the climax of my troubles centered on May of my senior year, the whole year was a shit show. The trouble had started elevating as I made my way through indoor soccer, and even if I wasn't getting arrested quite yet, I wasn't living to the standard that my parents had established. How I was living and how I was treating my parents, I was such an idiot. Looking back, I feel so bad about the way I treated my dad. He's 5-foot-8, not a big guy, doesn't have a temper and, even if he's been upset with me, he's never truly shown me anger. He's one of the best men I've ever met in my life. I remember several times being drunk out of my mind, screaming and trying to get him to react. I was looking for an altercation. Thank God it never got there.

Everybody likes that feeling of people seeing them do something great, particularly their parents. If you know me now, you know how much I love and care for my parents and how we have a great relationship. Looking back, I appreciated how much time they spent being at everything.

And so, as I scanned the crowd that day and didn't see them, it struck me. When I got home that night, I didn't ask where they were. But as the week wore on, with another game on the horizon, it was still eating at me. Their absence had thrown me off. Finally, the next game day arrived and I needed to know. "Hey, are you going to come to the game tonight?" I decided to ask my dad. He was blunt. "No, I'm not, Jason," I remember him saying. It was extremely painful to hear. "We're not happy with you right now," he said. I was hurt.

The indoor soccer seasons were short, and this one was nearing its end, but my parents didn't come to that next game or any of the rest. While my situation would worsen in the months ahead before my eventual wake-up call, this moment acted as an early jolt. For all this time it was like I couldn't hear or see my parents.

But it wasn't until this moment, when there was nobody there for me at soccer, nobody in the stands cheering me on, that I finally started hearing them. Everything I had done to this point hit me like a ton of bricks. Nothing had ever fazed me in terms of what my parents would say or the emotions they would show, but that particular moment of not seeing them in the stands and hearing my dad say, "No, we're not gonna be there." That one I definitely heard.

My parents were the ones who introduced me to soccer when I was 5 years old. At a young age they started putting me in everything just to see what I liked. One great thing about my parents is they were never pushy. They never told me I had to play this or do that. When I began playing soccer, they weren't screaming at me to do better or yelling at me to focus on the ball. My parents put me in positions and situations and watched to see if I liked it or not. So I tried everything. I played baseball, basketball, football and soccer. When you're that young, you don't know what you like, you like what you are good at. From the second I started playing soccer, I was really good at it. How could I not like it? I played primarily striker in soccer, but I'd get moved around, too. Sometimes my coach would put me at midfielder, allowing me to work all parts of the field. My claim to fame was taking a pass from the defense, maneuvering quickly through the opponent's half of the field and scoring. My speed really worked to my advantage. I loved it.

Living in West Texas, football was definitely king. We weren't far north of Odessa, Texas, home to the Permian Panthers of *Friday Night Lights*. All those stories about high school football in Texas are true. People live and breathe football all year long. I was into football, too. But for whatever reason, there was also a strong presence of soccer in Lubbock, Texas. There was this massive complex that seemed like it had 60 soccer fields, and we even had indoor soccer leagues, so when the regular season was over in the spring or fall, we'd keep playing indoors in the winter and summer. Soccer was my thing. At a young age, I was able to pick sports up very quickly, and it was impressive how I dominated. It wasn't until my teenage years when I finally felt like I had competition in soccer, when other kids started catching up with me. Until then, games would include me running around dominating the entire game, scoring 13, 14, 15 goals. Parents on the other sideline would get pissed off and start screaming. The parents on our own team would eventually get frustrated too. "Let's pull this guy out, he's dominating the game," I remember them yelling. "This isn't even a game." I loved soccer and how could I not?

I think my parents realized I was light years ahead of everybody else my age and on my team. That gap became most evident around middle school, which was also the same time I was beginning to be home-schooled. Because I wasn't in school and didn't have a social life, they lined me up to play on a select travel team, a very competitive soccer team called Excalibur. Our coach was a German man, Tom Messerschmidt, who played professionally for Bayern Munich before eventually settling in Lubbock. It was with Excalibur that I first met Greg. We hit it off immediately. During my three years with Excalibur we traveled all over the United States and played international teams as well. I had an incredible time. We'd practice all week and be gone playing games on the weekend. When we had any downtime, Greg and I would hang out. This is where my long spiral of trouble began. We were exploring with drugs and alcohol and chasing girls. I was still very focused on soccer. I loved the game, and I was flat-out good at it. At the tail end of my time with the travel team, my parents were approached about me trying out with an Olympic development program in Dallas, about a five-hour drive from Lubbock. While I was internally starting down a troublesome path, things were really pointing in the direction that I could and should play professional soccer. That's what Coach Messerschmidt told my parents. But near the end of playing for that team, as I was preparing to enter high school and 10th grade, is right when my life really began to go off the rails. That's when I was arrested for possession of marijuana, but it could have been worse. The amount of marijuana I had could have been classified "with intent to distribute," but it was knocked down to "possession." Still, that began my reckless behavior, which led to time in juvenile detention.

When I started my first year of high school, I went out for football. I had begun playing full contact football, as most Texas boys of that generation did, at 6 years old, and played every year for a team called the Raiders. Had I not been home-schooled, I would have definitely played tackle football for my junior high school in seventh and eighth grades. I love football, but it wasn't my main passion. I wasn't as dominating at football like I was at soccer.

When I returned to the public school system in ninth grade I did play football and I did really well on the field, but I wasn't very well-liked by teammates. I was suddenly inserted into this nucleus of kids who had been playing together for two years. But the real trouble for me was, truthfully, because I was so conditioned from soccer that I was showing other kids up. My club soccer team had worked our tails off all summer long playing in one of the biggest international soccer tournaments ever, in Pikes Peak, Colorado. We played at an altitude where it was hard to breathe, hard to run, and there were teams from across the United States and the United Kingdom. I think Coach Messerschmidt had a sense of, "I've got some good players on the team, but I don't have A+ players all the way down the bench." So to condition those of us he was going to lean on, he absolutely destroyed us with cardiovascular trainings. That meant, though, when I showed up for football two-a-days, I was in top-notch shape. Meanwhile, all these kids had been eating candy and hanging out by the pool all summer. I outperformed every person on that field during conditioning and the coach used me as leverage to try to motivate the players to go harder. At the same time, it drove a lot of resentment from these players that had been playing together. That led to me getting in altercations and trouble just as I was trying to get back into the school system.

After my arrest going into 10th grade, I went out for football and played as a kicker, cornerback and tailback. The team was incredibly structured, and the coaches were tough. These were West Texas coaches who smacked you with your own helmet when they were frustrated at you. They would literally punch in the locker while they were screaming at you. It was the type of stuff that wouldn't be politically correct enough to survive today. You hated them then, but looking back I respect that tough love, somebody roughing you up and screaming at you. My graduating class had more than 500 students, so there were a lot of kids on the football team. There were two or three practice squads so everyone could participate. If your grades weren't in line or if you got in trouble, you were more worried about getting reprimanded at practice than in the principal's office. Getting in trouble got me kicked off the team sometime by the end of 10th grade.

Soccer, for whatever reason, didn't have that structure. Our high school coach was a complete nut bag. He was pushing 70 years old, as crazy as it sounds. I don't know what war he was in, but he was definitely in a war. A plane would fly over the practice field and he'd scream, "They're back, they're back," and start running down the field shooting an imaginary gun at these planes. He was crazy, and we all laughed at him. You never knew who was going to show up—this fun, smiling, joking guy, or that guy with post-traumatic stress disorder. I lasted longer in high school soccer, because the soccer team wasn't quite as scrutinized. They weren't as strict on grades as the football team. The coach beat to his own drum and the school allowed it. There was nobody sending him grades and behavior reports. I remember being in trouble and I could still practice with the soccer team. And by that stage of my life, I was in trouble pretty much all the time.

AS I BEGAN MY 10TH GRADE year, my partying phase was taking over. I was having so much fun that I didn't really care what happened. On the high school soccer team I should have easily been considered a star, but I was in such frequent trouble that I could never become one. My focus had shifted to doing all the things that were getting me in trouble rather than staying clean so I could play Friday night in the soccer game. And somehow that didn't bother me. For the first time since I kicked a ball, soccer was suddenly not important, and eventually I was kicked off the soccer team, too. I was addicted to how fun it was to be partying.

I can imagine lots of things that could have, maybe would have, happened in my life if I had not been introduced to drugs and alcohol at such a young age. You could argue I could have gone on to play professional soccer. But the power and the draw of the party life took over. It was all I craved. At that point in my life any sort of punishment wasn't meaningful to me. Parents often try to take away or leverage things that matter to their kids. That wasn't possible for me because soccer was my last hot button. Threatening me with it no longer worked. While I was kicked off the high school soccer team, I was still able to play soccer—Greg and I would play in the summer indoor league that had nothing to do with the school system and I played in other non-school related leagues, too—I didn't play as much and I wasn't conditioning myself as much or fine-tuning my skills with a coach. But I was still out there playing, which would lead to the chance to play soccer at Texas Tech University a few years down the road. But during this window, I was starting to harden into this wannabe badass little shit with no respect for anybody.

There are a lot of what-ifs in life. And sometimes the what-if that takes you down a different road is of your own making. Soccer could have been my path, but I disrupted that. I've chosen to believe the Lord helped me get a whole series of disruptors out of my system early so that I might one day find a new sport...one called business.

CHAPTER 4

A New Sport: Direct Sales & AdvoCare

My introduction to direct sales began with a bit of disbelief. It had been about a year and a half since I had abandoned my destructive ways. I was in college at Texas Tech University and, for all intents and purposes, I was conforming to society and becoming the person my parents hoped I would be. I still remember hanging out with some friends when, somehow, someway, one of them made a comment about an old friend.

"Yeah, Wes Bewley, he just got a new Corvette," they told me. There was no way, I thought. Wes and I had become friends through soccer, but he wasn't a destructive person like I was. He was a big-time track athlete and our childhood houses had been close together, so we had a history. "He can't afford a Corvette," I responded. "Yeah," one of my friends said, "I just saw him in a brand-new Corvette." This caught my attention.

The one thing you need to know about me is, outside of those canned cinnamon rolls my dad used to wake me up with, there was no greater desire in my life than cars.

Ever since I knew what a car was, or anything that was powerful for that matter, I was hooked. Dirt bikes, four-wheelers, it didn't matter. From the moment I knew what a sports car was I thought they were the coolest thing on Earth. Of course, in Lubbock, Texas, we didn't have any exotic cars. There were no Ferraris, no Lamborghinis. Growing up, I'd go to the grocery store with my parents and buy a little model kit of a Lamborghini and put it together. But you'd never see anything like it in real life. What we did have in Lubbock was a car dealership called Classic Motor Cars, which was 90 percent Corvettes and 10 percent muscle cars like Firebirds, Mustangs and Cobras that were tricked out with aftermarket exhaust, super-wide wheels on the back and racing stripes. They had all years and models of Corvettes and only had the best of the best in their inventory. Anything Classic Motor Cars had was killer.

My dad knew I loved cars, so once a week, maybe even twice a week, whenever he wasn't pissed off at me or I did something good or he just felt like being a good dad, he would take me to Classic Motor Cars. My dad hated car salesmen, but the dealership was probably five miles from our house, and we'd go at night when they were closed. I wanted to go all the time. "Dad," I'd say, "we should go to Classic Motors Cars, maybe something new came in." That's what started my colossal dreaming of cars and this crazy desire to have them. All of them. It ended up torturing my dad when I started getting a driver's license, because I had this audacious demand about what I wanted, which was obviously unrealistic. My dad gave me his Ford Ranger as my first vehicle, and I was utterly disappointed. But the one thing I was good at back then, and it has stuck with me to this day, is being relentless. My Ford Ranger was fine. But finally, after months of persistent pestering, I broke my dad down. I needed something cooler. That something was a used Chevy

T-Top Camaro. It wasn't the newest, it wasn't the fastest and he refused to get me a V8 engine, but nonetheless I had something that, in my mind, was cool.

When I heard Wes had a brand-new Corvette, I didn't believe it. By the time I got home from hanging out with my friends, it was already midnight. It was really late for adults, but not for college kids, so I called Wes' house. His mom answered. "Is Wes there?" I asked. "No, he's not," she responded. "Who's calling?" I made up a name. I felt bad because it was so late. Two days later, Wes called me. "Hey, did you call my house?" he asked. It must have been on Caller ID because he knew I had called.

"Yeah, I heard you got a Corvette," I said. "Yeah, I did," he told me. I was stunned. "You're kidding me," I said. "How in the world could you afford it?" His answer would begin my journey into direct sales and where I am today. "Well, remember that thing I told you about like a year and a half ago?" he asked me. Everything began to make sense. That was all I needed to hear. As soon as I heard or saw that what he was doing could lead to me getting a car like that is when I said "Go time" in terms of focus, intensity and working. "We've got to meet," I told him. "We've got to meet now."

I had run into Wes at the Lubbock mall during the summer about a year and a half earlier. I was attempting to stay off the radar after my string of senior-year arrests and was starting to turn things around. Wes was so excited when he saw me. He had these products he wanted to tell me about. I had never been introduced to direct sales and I had no idea what was going on. I heard in his voice how excited he was. I casually listened as he went on and on. I didn't know what exactly was going on and had no idea why he was telling me about these products. When he was done rambling, Wes asked me to come to his mom's house. His parents were divorced and it was the house he had mostly grown up in not far from my house. When I walked in, Wes made me this drink filled with caffeine. Growing up in my super conservative family, a pop tart was my biggest treat. My mom was strict. She was all about vegetables and no sugar. Looking back, that was probably what helped me perform so well in athletics and helped lead to my healthy lifestyle now, but back then it sucked. So when Wes gave me this drink, it was the first time I ever had a caffeine drink in my life. After he gave me this caffeinated drink, he popped in a VHS tape about the products. I remember sitting there watching this video and this caffeine drink hit me like a bolt of lightning. I wanted to run around his house. That was my introduction to the entire direct sales industry and the unknowing start to my Thrivin' journey.

I went home that night with plans to get started. It was $40 to get a distributor kit, so I asked my dad for help. My dad was a very supportive person, but he was conservative with his money. He probably thought this was a flash in the pan, but I was also back on a good track in life and had my head on my shoulders. So my dad wrote me a $40 check for the distributor kit. When it arrived at my house, it sat in the corner. I forgot about the company, distributor kit and Wes for a year or so. Wes, on the other hand, had taken off. When I heard about his new Corvette, that forgotten distributor kit was quickly dusted off, and I was ready to do whatever it took to make it happen like Wes had.

Wes had been introduced to AdvoCare by a guy I called Danny Mac. Wes coached summer track at Texas Tech, and Danny's kids were in Wes' track clinic that summer. Most parents would drop their kids off and go to work, but Danny would pull up with a new fancy car every day. He showed up wearing gym clothes and would sit in the bleachers and watch the clinic. Wes was always intrigued. One day he asked Danny what he did for a living. "I'll tell you tomorrow." The next day Danny returned with a book, *Rich Dad, Poor Dad*, and had torn a $100 bill in half. He stuck one half in the book and said, "Read the book and I'll give you the other half of this $100 bill and I'll tell you what I do for a living. If I tell you now it won't make sense to you."

Danny had an incredible success story. He had been a high school football coach in Prosper, Texas. He was completely broke, in Chapter 13 bankruptcy, when he discovered AdvoCare. He and his wife, Diane, had grinded from the bottom up. When he ran into Wes at the summer clinic, Danny was making $150,000 a month and was the top person in AdvoCare. He was very polished, sharp and had all the right things to say. Wes had come from a loving but divorced family. I always felt like Wes had a bit of a "missing dad" element in his life. He grew up in Lubbock with his mom and he'd go see his dad in the summers. He spent a couple years of high school with his dad before coming back to Lubbock, but it seemed there was a missing piece in his life. I felt like Wes saw Danny as a father figure. When Wes met Danny, he quickly met Diane, he saw the boys that he was coaching at track and he saw this beautiful, picture-perfect American family. Danny also had cool cars. He had one of the first Dodge Vipers when they came out, and there was no cooler car, especially in Lubbock. But that wasn't the major connector for Wes. He was seeing a family that needed nothing from a financial perspective and the togetherness of perfection. That was the hook in Wes' mouth.

Wes read the book and was introduced to Danny and this world of AdvoCare and direct selling. I don't know what Danny told Wes after Wes read the book and got the other half of that $100 bill, but it was definitely something creative and witty. Danny was a wordsmith and well put together. Whatever he told Wes lit Wes' world up as did the book. Hearing this story from Wes led me to read *Rich Dad, Poor Dad*, which was one of the first books I ever *wanted* to read. I hated school. I wasn't good at it. I'm really good at math and coming up with calculations in my head, but school never interested me. My parents finally came to that realization when I was being home-schooled. This was the first book I ever read that I was excited to read. I soaked it all in. I didn't meet Danny in person for a couple of months, but I spoke to him on the phone within the first week of me deciding mentally, "Ok, this is it." No joking around. I'm pushing all my chips in. Go-time.

Wes gave me the rundown on AdvoCare and what I needed to do to be successful not long after our phone call about his new Corvette. It was pretty simple. "We're looking for customers that want to buy these products and we're looking for people that want to sell them," was the message. It was the old-school sales thought process. Let's put your list together. Who do you know? With whom do you have credibility? It wasn't easy for me. I was essentially coming out of rehab. I had just reformed myself, so the people that I did know I didn't really want to be associated with. Plus, I didn't have a ton of credibility with the right people. That was a huge hurdle. In a short span I went from drugs, partying, troubles with the law to now selling vitamins. That was a big problem. It was tough getting started. I spent more time in meetings and on conference calls gaining knowledge than I did physically trying to go out there and talk to people. It's not that I didn't want to, I just didn't have a lot of people to talk to.

I remember trying to talk to my good old buddy Greg Bernstein about it. Like me, Greg thought cars were really cool. He had a brand new Pontiac Trans-Am. He and I were intrigued by Wes and we both liked the idea of what Wes had quickly accomplished. Wes was already making $3,000-$5,000 a month. That's a lot of money for someone who's 20 years old. There was intrigue from Greg about the AdvoCare business, but there was no "eye of the tiger" spirit with Greg like there was with me. Greg was a little younger and was still in school. For Greg it was, "Ok, this is cool. This shiny object is cool." For me it was different: "I'm going to go tear this thing apart and go get me a Corvette." Greg's dad eventually said "Yes" just to support Greg. There were three packages that AdvoCare sold. One was $375, one was $1,500 and one was $2,100. Greg's dad gave him money for the lowest package. That was my first sell. Nothing ever materialized for Greg. I would frequently see his dad at the local gym in town, and I remember him telling me how much he was enjoying the products. The products were supposed to be used for Greg to get going with his business, and I think his dad essentially ate the supply. I was just getting started.

I dropped out of Texas Tech to pursue AdvoCare. I didn't know what I wanted to do in college anyway. I saw AdvoCare as a great opportunity. I felt I wasn't learning anything applicable in college. Meanwhile, it felt like I was getting really educated on life via AdvoCare. I was learning how real life and finance worked. I was always an athlete, I liked business and being successful. Soccer was gone, but direct sales and business quickly replaced it. That turned into my sport. There were so many life lessons I learned with AdvoCare. I met a lot of people that said a lot of meaningful things at an early age. They weren't necessarily speaking directly to me, but I could hear them. Seeing the lifestyle that they were living, people making $40,000, $50,000 and $60,000 up to Danny making $150,000 a month and not having to go into an actual J.O.B. I started learning there was an alternate life, that there was a way to live that was totally different than anything and everything I had ever known. I related to this because I always wanted something different.

I had some success for someone who was as young as I was. I made $2,000 per month on average with an occasional $4,000 month sprinkled in. It certainly wasn't enough to be considered a success, but I was able to pay bills here and there and keep things afloat with my nominal expenses in Lubbock. Wes, on the other hand, was this bright kid who was also extremely young, but was super successful and showcasing his Corvette around Texas Tech, selling a lot of products to girls who wanted to lose weight or fraternity guys who had dad's credit card. I didn't have the Corvette to go flaunting around like that and even if I did, Wes was always better at the recruiting aspect of things. I wasn't good at cold calling. I think of my time in Lubbock as my boot camp in direct sales.

When I look back, what I remember most prominently about my time then was how bad I wanted to succeed in AdvoCare. I couldn't have wanted it more. I couldn't have been any more dedicated. I couldn't have been any more determined. It wasn't for lack of effort. I checked off all the boxes you'd need to succeed in direct sales: Is this person committed? Are they determined? Are they sacrificing? Check, check, check. All my chips were pushed in. I didn't have the big win, but I wanted it so bad. When an opportunity to move to Nashville, Tennessee, with Wes and other AdvoCare leaders popped up, it felt like it made a lot of sense. "Ok, this is the next step in the AdvoCare journey," I thought. There was certainly some fear of loss. People I had admired, looked up to and considered very smart, sharp, successful people in AdvoCare were moving without me if I didn't go. If they were all doing it, it had to be the right decision. It felt like the AdvoCare movement in Lubbock was winding down.

CHAPTER 5

Was This Whole Thing a Mistake?

During my years with AdvoCare in Lubbock, the company was really taking off nationally. They had just signed a big deal with the Tennessee Titans' Steve McNair, who was their new hot quarterback. There was an initiative to open AdvoCare in a new section of the country. It was the next chapter. Everybody was so excited. We had seen what had happened in the Southwest and now we had the hottest professional quarterback in the country at that time on our magazine and Nashville was declared our new frontier.

That was the lure in the water. Wes and I had become roommates in Lubbock, and I remember Wes coming to me and delivering the news. "I'm moving to Nashville," he told me. "There's this big group coming together. Danny's moving out there too. You should come. We'll get out there, we'll blow up our businesses, we'll get to be around Danny nonstop." Anything Danny Mac did in life Wes did at this point. But Wes was right. Lubbock was one small piece of AdvoCare. The company was looking east. At that time AdvoCare was primarily a Texas and Oklahoma company and there was no such thing as e-commerce. In those days you called in your orders or faxed them, and the business stuck where the nucleus of people were. In Nashville, Wes said, we could leverage the opportunity and go grow our businesses in a part of the country that was untouched. It made sense.

Everything felt right about the move other than me not having a lot of money. I was hesitant to move to Nashville, but it didn't scare me. I've never been a risk-averse person, but Lubbock I knew. Still, trading comfort for opportunity is what has always allowed the great ones to make a name for themselves. I was ready to make my name in AdvoCare.

I still believed that I could find more success in direct sales like Danny and all these other people I saw living their dream life. It was always right there. I had to keep going. I was never discouraged. Part of what kept moving me forward is I have really thick skin, which I didn't know at the time. I thought everybody was a fighter in life. I thought you decided you were going to go do something and that's what you did. No matter what happened, you just kept fighting. I was a determined and strong-willed person. I may not have been the best looking or the most educated, but dammit there were very few in the room that were going to out-fight and out-work me. I had to get to the next level. My car I wanted was there. My lifestyle I wanted was there. Once I started meeting all these people that were making a lot of money and had "life on their terms" as they always referred to it, I started getting educated at an extremely young age on what I really wanted. I wasn't making money yet. So what? I felt like success was right there within my grasp. Just make another phone call. Just talk to one more person.

WES AND I MOVED TO NASHVILLE and rented a place together. For a while, it was great. AdvoCare moved the majority of their field leadership to Nashville and a lot of people followed from Texas. You could see the expansion in Tennessee, Alabama and Kentucky. The whole Nashville area absolutely ignited. On a personal level, Wes was right. We did get to spend a lot of time learning from Danny Mac. I had been around Danny and his wife probably 15 times when I was in Lubbock. Danny would frequently come conduct a large group meeting in a hotel and everybody came to town. It was a big deal when Danny was there. Afterward he would do an invitation-only training. Wes was someone who Danny took under his wing early, and I was Wes' guy. As a result, Danny started taking a liking to me, as well. I think it was because he saw the fire in my eyes. My time with Danny increased exponentially in Nashville. I was probably with him once and sometimes twice a week. Whether it was training, a motivational talk, small group sessions, large group meetings, we were always doing something. I met a lot of people in Nashville, but nobody talked like Danny. He thought and spoke on another level and he took extra time to encourage me. I'm naturally a dreamer, but I am also a doer. He was very much in that mindset, and I learned a lot from him.

What I cherish most about my time with AdvoCare is the people I met and what I learned. The first half of my time with AdvoCare in Lubbock I learned the mechanics of how to build a sales organization, how to go get customers, how to get distributors, how to recruit, how to train. It was really a crash course in how you build a direct sales organization. In Nashville, when I was with Danny and his top leaders, their training wasn't really about the mechanics of how to go talk to a customer. It was big picture: Here's how you become a leader in life. I'd never heard anybody talk like that. I had gone to school my whole life; I had gone to church my whole life. Everybody told me in church what the Bible said and in school the teachers were always talking about a particular subject. Danny and his leaders were talking about life lessons and adversity and peaks and valleys and how to look at life differently. It was the foundational knowledge on what becoming a success is about, how you lead people, what being a leader means. It set me up to go on to where I am today in my life and career. It was a perfect start. The training was unbelievable. I still have all these journals of notes taken from my time there. When I do training on the importance of journals I tell people, "Look, I have three journals here that have led to billions of dollars in sales." That's how I view it.

What I learned in AdvoCare was absolutely priceless, and it was the foundational steppingstone to groom me and get started in this industry. If you go in the military, they don't simply put a gun in your hand and throw you on the front line. They train you, they condition you, and most importantly, they get your freaking mind right. They get you to view situations the way they know you need to view them, and the way you should view them, to get you home safe. That's what AdvoCare was for me. It was a boot camp of foundational knowledge upon which I built the rest of my success.

My success didn't come at AdvoCare though. Wes was right about pretty much everything he told me regarding the move to Nashville minus our business exploding in a positive way. My business dropped and I made less money. At AdvoCare, the desire and passion to go get it, to make it happen, a span of eight years, had me doing crazy things. I remember walking around mall parking lots and trying to talk to people, going to their car and putting fliers on windshields. I would put fliers up on apartment mailboxes. At the bottom of the sheet of paper were 10 slits with my phone number that people could rip off. I would pre-rip off eight of them and leave only two so people would think it was in high demand. I thought I was so smart. None of that ever worked.

I was living off peanut butter and jelly sandwiches and canned tuna that I could buy for 79 cents. I had my head hung low and my tail between my legs. I had absolutely zero confidence whatsoever in my ability, who I was or what I could accomplish. I had no idea what to do. When I started with AdvoCare my dad always told me, "There's nothing you should be ashamed of if you end up having to go get a job while you're growing your AdvoCare business." I didn't want to do that. I wanted to devote everything I had to making it work. AdvoCare was not a part-time goal to me.

One of the things I felt early was that to project success, I couldn't have a job and then do AdvoCare on the side. To people I was trying to recruit, it would scream that I was not doing well. When I met people, I never lied or tried to portray something different, but I felt like there was clout and I saw eyes open up a little more when I said I did this full time. (Little did they know I was completely broke!) It was bad enough, in my mind, that I didn't have fancy cars and some of the other window dressing that caught people's attention.

When I moved to Nashville my dad handed me a credit card and told me to use it only for the direst of emergencies. "This is not play money," he told me. "This is if you have a true emergency and you can't get a hold of me." The credit card limit was only $5,000, and I wasn't making money. That meant everything was an emergency in my eyes. I could barely afford to put gas in my car and I had to budget $8 to go to Walmart and get my tuna and peanut butter and jelly sandwiches. I remember calling Capital One over and over during that period. I knew my dad's social security number and date of birth, so I'd act like him and ask for a credit increase. I eventually got it raised to $25,000. For a while, I was able to pay the minimum balance. Then the minimum became $600. Then $700. At the time, I was still on this mission in life to become successful and pay back my parents for all the damage I felt like I had caused in my earlier years. I owed them, but here I was causing more harm.

Having reached the point where I could no longer afford the monthly minimum payments, I decided to come clean to my dad. Like with my troubles in high school, he wasn't mad. He didn't shout or scream. "Jason, I had no idea you were in this bad of shape. You should have told me. You should have communicated with me," he said. "We thought you were working and doing good things with AdvoCare and everything was great." I'm not a person who asks for help. I just try to figure it out. But I was running out of options. My parents had put aside some money for college, and since I never finished, my dad said he would pay off the credit card and I could make payments to him instead. He had always taught me you don't live life in debt, a lesson I've come to appreciate. I started making dinky payments of $50 here and $100 there. The payments were inconsistent, but I was determined that I would get a hit one day soon and pay my dad back.

Back in Nashville, it was becoming increasingly apparent that hit wasn't going to come with AdvoCare. When the company's focus first shifted to Nashville it was on a true upward trajectory. But shortly after the move, the founder of AdvoCare, Charlie Ragus, died. He had been the backbone of the company. He was a true leadership figurehead, he was AdvoCare. He was one of those people that when he entered a room, everyone stopped because he was so well respected. When he took the stage, people shut up. He had a very strong presence and energy about him. He always said, "Your leadership's got to be as strong as a bear's breath." He wasn't that leader who lived in the shadows while the executive team ran the company. When he passed away it was a complete shock. Other leaders took the flag and the company was on the rebound from his passing when an even bigger blow came: the Food and Drug Administration banned the stimulant ephedra. It was the most important ingredient in AdvoCare's top weight loss product, Metabolic Orange. When Metabolic Orange was pulled off the market, I remember being told AdvoCare went from sales of $370 million annually to $70 million. It all happened in about 12-15 months. That's when everything started collapsing.

I don't blame my sales troubles at AdvoCare on those events, but it was tough on the company and my business. The numbers on everybody's checks were dropping like a bad stock market. I was making $2,000 a month previously. Suddenly, the number was near zero.

One thing you'll find is true for me is that I'm big on reflection. You'll read it throughout this book and hopefully hear it in any conversation we might have. Whether something turns out poorly or even if it is a home run, I look back and seek lessons learned. I've always felt it was the best education.

When I look back at why I never found success at AdvoCare I come to a few conclusions. When you're that young, you don't have a ton of credibility with people, and the people that you do have credibility with—many of them near your own age—aren't necessarily the movers and shakers in life. It seemed like people that did well and excelled weren't in their early 20s. Being able to grow and succeed in direct sales is like building a football team, and I couldn't find a damn quarterback. I brought in so many people. I worked the business like crazy and for whatever reason I just wasn't able to make it happen. Looking back now, the tale of Jason Camper wasn't to be successful in AdvoCare. My time in AdvoCare was a learning ground in the industry and life itself. My destiny in AdvoCare wasn't to make money. But it was to give me the knowledge to go to the next level.

I remember the day I called Wes to tell him I was done with AdvoCare, that I couldn't do it anymore. I was eternally grateful to Wes. He was the person that introduced me to this industry. How could I not be grateful? Wes answered the phone and I began an almost apologetic goodbye. "Hey, I just want to let you know I'm done, brother. It's not going to happen for me," I told him. "I've got to go elsewhere, I gave it my all." Wes didn't say much. I remember closing the call by encouraging him to press on. "Don't ever give up, Wes, you've got something going and I'm going to be cheering for you all the way and you guys are just incredible, you've done so much for me," I said. "I wish it wasn't like this, but I can't live off canned tuna and a hidden credit card from my dad the rest of my life."

I thought I had said goodbye correctly, but what really hurt was how, almost immediately, everybody at AdvoCare cut me off. AdvoCare at that time was filled with leaders who had the attitude of, "You're either with us or against us." The relationships I had built for years were gone overnight. Other than Wes, who I reconciled with years later, I've talked to very few of those people ever again. There were hundreds of relationships gone with just one call. That left a bad taste in my mouth. I probably wanted to succeed at AdvoCare more than anybody that has ever signed up in the history of the company. I don't know if I could have wanted it more and I was still their biggest cheerleader. Heck, it wasn't as if I was going to a competitor. I was simply trying to figure my life out and what I was going to do and how I might pay my bills. And there was an attitude of, "Well, you're against us now." I was out.

Nashville was bittersweet for me. At the time it was all bitter, but it has become bittersweet as I look back on that struggle and that hardship. I lived in a completely ridiculous apartment that I called the "Matchbox" because it felt like I was this little mouse that lived inside. I lived off peanut butter and tuna. To this day you'll still see me eating tuna, not because I like it but because I did it for so long that it's ingrained in me. What I learned was invaluable. My time there was all about leadership and life lessons. So while it was very bitter at the time and there were an insane amount of hardships, and it was a very dark period in my life, what I learned through AdvoCare was priceless. Even to this day, I have nothing but the utmost respect for those relationships.

I view my time at AdvoCare in two chapters. The first chapter was my time in Lubbock learning Direct Selling 101. The second chapter in Nashville was filled with many lessons. In all my time with the company barely scraping by to make commissions, and then to hardly making nothing and living off tuna. I don't know if I made $160,000 in eight years. But I wouldn't trade the experience for 100 times that money. It was a devastating moment for me when I finally let go of AdvoCare. It felt like I was letting someone I loved fall off the edge of the cliff. Every month, I swear to you, I truly believed I was just on the verge of a breakthrough…at least that's the narrative I told myself. Everyone around me was finding success and Wes' business continued to grow. I was with what I felt was the best company at AdvoCare, and I thought if I couldn't make it happen there, I had no shot of making it happen anywhere in direct sales. I got out of the industry, and as far as I knew, I was done with direct selling. I had no idea then that it was grooming me for the next level in my life and eventually to where I am today.

Years later, a company that I had always respected and viewed so eloquently and had ironically become a competitor of mine, ran into trouble with federal regulators and changed its business model. The AdvoCare today is not the AdvoCare that it once was.

CHAPTER 6

Rediscovering Direct Sales & Burn Lounge

When I finally left AdvoCare, I was mentally exhausted. Despite all the lessons I later realized I had learned during my experience there, I had no interest right then in direct sales. I stayed in Nashville and started waiting tables and, as crazy as it sounds, I found happiness with that.

I was a waiter in an artsy part of Nashville at a boutique restaurant called the Yellow Porch. They had a fancy chef who cooked up all kinds of off-the-wall dishes. It wasn't a very big spot at all, and I didn't have any big restaurant experience, so they would only let me work lunch, leaving the more prestigious night shift to the veteran waiters. It was a high-end place, and the customers seemed to have money. I remember how good it felt to actually have cash in my pocket. My electric bill came and I could actually pay it. I would make between $50 and $70 waiting tables during lunch time, and sometimes made $100 on a great, fantastic day. It wasn't a lot, but I finally had some money to do things and I never had to wonder if or when I might get paid. Being the motivated and driven person I am financially and putting two and two together, I decided if I was going to wait tables I wanted to be at a restaurant where the biggest tab was being spent by each customer. That way, my tip would be bigger, too.

I found that more upscale job at Fleming's Steakhouse and, to my luck, the hiring manager, Grant, knew what AdvoCare was. He thought it was the coolest thing that I had worked with them for so long. He knew how hard direct sales was and he was an athletic guy's guy, like myself. He seemed to like me the second I walked into the interview. I had no business being in this caliber of restaurant. I fibbed on my application about my wine knowledge and might have exaggerated what I knew from the Yellow Porch. Grant probably saw right through me, but we seemed to click. He helped me get the job and taught me about wine. I took things really seriously, and my wine knowledge went through the roof, helping me sell wine to customers. It quickly paid off. I went from making $50 a day at Yellow Porch to around $300 a night at Fleming's Steakhouse. I was starting to get back on my feet, able to catch up on bills and started kicking some money off to my dad.

As nice as it was to be earning the money I was at Fleming's, I also knew I couldn't spend the rest of my life in a restaurant and was on the lookout for something more career oriented. Shortly after, I was introduced to a gentleman by the name of Brandon Sandefur, who owned Evergreen Mortgage. I remember him coming into Fleming's and telling me how much money I could make. "I've got these guys making $200,000 a year," he bragged. "We're going through this refinance boom." I was sucked back into the dreams of financial success that had driven me before. I left Fleming's for another dream.

There were people making real money at Evergreen and I met good people there, but it wasn't everything Brandon said it was going to be. I was given a big lead list of people who had shown interest in refinancing their house and I was left to start cold calling. I made money at Evergreen, but I was back on the rollercoaster that caused so much turmoil at AdvoCare. The money I had been making at Fleming's was steady, $300 a night like clockwork. No matter what, I knew I was going to walk out of the restaurant with cash. When I went to do mortgages at Evergreen, I might make $4,000 a month, or I might make zero based on how many home closings I had.

I was able to pay bills but the fear and pain that I had endured for so long at AdvoCare returned. You didn't know when your next commission was going to show up and never felt like you could spend your check when it did come because you weren't sure how long it would need to last. Even if I had a big month at Evergreen and made a $3,000 commission, I was scared to spend it, go eat, do anything, because I knew next month could be $0. I found it difficult to string together successful months and I learned that the guys in the office who were making $100,000 or more had been there for years and had long lists of Realtors and insurance agents they could lean on for deal flow. They weren't sitting in the office making cold calls like I was. They'd take their connections to Happy Hours and kick around referrals.

The job quickly became another commission-based job that didn't pan out, and I was back on tuna and peanut butter and jelly sandwiches pretty quickly. I stayed at Evergreen for about a year, and while I was only there a short period of time, I felt like I received a finance degree within six months. I learned a ton about finance, which helped me as an executive later on.

There was one other big positive of my time at Evergreen. Whenever I did feel OK spending $20 or $30 on a meal, my best friend, Jason Cullers, and I would go to Bonefish Grill, which wasn't far from my apartment. We were single guys working in Nashville, living life and trying to have fun. We loved the appetizers at Bonefish and grabbing a beer. One Saturday night while I was at a local bar having a drink with a friend, I noticed a girl who was the bartender I always saw at Bonefish. I approached her. "Hey, you work at Bonefish. I love that place, I go there all the time," I told her, "Yes I do, my name is Tracy…Tracy Jones," she said. Tracy and I talked for a while that night, getting to know each other. We didn't exchange contact information, but I told her I would come see her at Bonefish soon. And the next week I did. I happened to leave my wallet at the bar. The next morning I got to the office at Evergreen and had a voicemail. "Hey, this is Tracy, I have your wallet. Your business card was in there so that's how I got your phone number," she said. "I can bring you your wallet if you need me to." Around lunchtime, Tracy brought my wallet over and asked if I wanted to go to lunch at a nearby Japanese restaurant. The funny thing was, Tracy and I had both moved to Nashville in pursuit of a job. She had moved from Orlando. When I met her, she was regional corporate trainer for Bonefish helping the new restaurants in the area open and train staff. It was a new chapter in her life, moving somewhere different, doing something different. They were the same reasons I had moved to Nashville for AdvoCare. I didn't consider our lunch really a date, but it would be the start of a long relationship and marriage. So you have to consider this window of my life EXTREMELY successful, even if it wasn't financially so!

To this day Tracy still thinks I left my wallet at her bar intentionally. Maybe I did!

I ENDED UP LEAVING EVERGREEN not long after I met Tracy when that calling toward direct sales came knocking again. I hadn't touched direct sales for roughly three years when Park Weatherly called me. I had worked with Park at AdvoCare while I was in Lubbock. He called to tell me that he, too, was leaving AdvoCare and there was a large group of people that no longer worked there who were at this new startup company, Burn Lounge. He told me, "It's a truly unique concept." When I took a look, I had never seen anything like it.

Burn Lounge had partnered with Sony, BMG and some other record labels and built their own digital music website. It was like what iTunes has become today. You could search for a song and buy it, and even buy an entire album. Nobody had done anything like it at that time. It was right about the time of Napster and mp3 players and nobody had any idea where the space was headed. Apple hadn't even announced its first iPod yet. But everyone was beginning to see that there was this new frontier of digital media happening. Everybody saw you could download music and knew it was only a matter of time before you could download a movie. And here was this new company, Burn Lounge.

It was a super cool concept. It couldn't be any cooler. Plus, it was backed by big names. Several celebrities had invested in it. In the time since I had worked at AdvoCare I had convinced myself I was never going to be successful in direct sales and had forgotten about the industry. I don't know if it's because Burn Lounge seemed so different or because it was such a different conversation, but I said "Yes" pretty quickly. One caveat: this time, I took my dad's advice from when I first started at AdvoCare. I said "Yes," but with a toe in the water. I didn't quit my job at Evergreen, but I did start slowly, casually calling people I knew. It was so much easier. I was simply sharing my new music store with people and trying to get them to buy songs off the website. Unlike AdvoCare, Burn Lounge exploded for me. As Burn Lounge started taking off and showing signs of being the real deal, I quit Evergreen. "I'm going all-in with this direct sales thing another time," I decided.

The success at Burn Lounge happened quick. Within six months, things were (figuratively) on fire. I was legitimately having success, and I remember these light bulbs coming on for me amidst my run with the company. "Oh my gosh, I am good enough," I thought. "I am good enough to succeed in this industry. It wasn't me. I thought it was me the whole time." My experience at AdvoCare had beaten me up and devastated me so much that I was convinced that it was me, that I was the problem. When it became apparent that I was very good at this and I quickly built a huge, successful team, I started noticing things. I noticed I had leadership abilities like I used during my sports career. I was always a leader, and this was the first time where I saw my leadership abilities flourish in business.

And it was paying off financially. The compensation plan was much different than AdvoCare. Burn Lounge had only two legs of business, which was a newer concept, a binary compensation plan. Basically, it worked like this: If I sign you up, that's one leg. If I sign up Kate, she's two. If I sign up Paige as my third person, I've got to put her underneath one of the first two. From there, you have to keep the volume well-balanced to receive commission. If you have this giant leg on one side, and you don't have anything on the other side, you don't get paid.

I became one of the most talked about people in the company because my business was growing so fast. I was making substantial income quickly, at one point averaging $17,000 a week. I traveled all over the country. I built a huge, successful team and met a ton of people. It was an extremely fun experience; everything was going so well. Then it all came crashing down.

Remember that unique binary comp plan and unique business model? The Federal Trade Commission wasn't as enamored with them. With no warning to the sales force, the FTC got a judge to approve a temporary restraining order on the company. Burn Lounge was shut down overnight. Everything I had built, all the success I was finally having, was gone. I had just started looking at building a home in Nashville. It seemed like everything was coming together for me and this dream of being able to build this large six-figure, seven-figure career felt real. Everything was finally working. I had the tiger by the tail, and in the blink of the eye, it was all gone.

Burn Lounge was deemed a pyramid scheme and their compensation plan was deemed illegal. What seemed to really hurt Burn Lounge was the novel business model. It was flat-out misunderstood. It was like, "Oh, my God, we've never seen a tiger with this kind of stripes before. We don't even know if this is a tiger, we're not sure how to classify it." When you are a misunderstood business model, and on top of that you aren't checking all the boxes, regulators aren't generally fans. That's what did Burn Lounge in. The comp plan proved to be the biggest sticking point for the FTC. They hated the binary. It turned direct sales into more of a recruiting business with no real customer. On top of that, it was a completely new idea. Burn Lounge was one of the first companies ever where you were essentially selling someone a web package. When someone got started in AdvoCare, if they paid $500, they received $500 in product. At Burn Lounge you were essentially selling a website. There wasn't a tangible product, which wasn't totally understood at the time. There was too much uncertainty, and that caused the FTC to start pursuing and building a case. It didn't help that once they started building a case they saw how poorly managed the company was. Now the narrative became, "You're different, which doesn't necessarily make you bad, but not only are you different, you're also not a T-crosser or an I-dotter." Burn Lounge was going 80 mph on a 60 mph freeway, and everything came collapsing down.

And I was standing there, crushed.

WHAT WAS SO DISHEARTENING was how Burn Lounge went down with no warning from the company's management. Executives who knew this might be coming said nothing to those of us who were busting our butts, leaving us to clean up the damage done to all the people working to make the place a success. There were people whose livelihoods depended on the company, and there was never any indication anything might be awry. With the snap of a finger and no indication of a cloudy day on the horizon, much less a Category 5 hurricane, these folks running the company allowed us to be walloped. Everything was gone. The company was shut down. We couldn't access the website. We weren't getting paid.

Just a week prior I had been on a call with the company's vice president and he went on and on about how incredible my team was growing, how it was the fastest growing one at the company and a year from now I could be this or that. It couldn't be any better. I was killing it. Then we just had mud on our faces. I remember enrolling people just a day before everything got shut down. Can you imagine? You're talking to someone about how good a company this is, and they give you their credit card and tell you they're in. The next day the company's out of business.

I still remember one of those last clients, Chuck. I had met him at my local gym in Franklin, Tennessee, just outside of Nashville. He was a corporate America class act, 6-foot, late 40s, traditional looking American guy. He wasn't the type of person who would touch direct sales. For one, he made high six figures. And then he had an attitude that he didn't need direct sales. When I presented Burn Lounge to Chuck, he found it so unique that it didn't really look like, smell like or feel like traditional network marketing. It had big-name celebrity investors for God's sake! Still, Chuck never would have said "Yes" to Burn Lounge had it not been me and my credibility and my influence on him. He finally said, "Yes, Jason, I'll give it a go," just a few days before the FTC came calling. That was one of the toughest calls I've ever made. Chuck was someone that I had really respected and someone I saw as a classy individual. And while Chuck wasn't mad or irate with me, the trust was obviously broken. Who he thought I was as a person, that image and his assessment of me, it was almost like that was completely gone, like he was wrong about me.

I felt so guilty about the people who put their trust in me—and backed it up with their money—that I started reaching into my own pocket to give certain folks refunds.

The suddenness of Burn Lounge's demise left a lot of questions. What happened? Did we do something? Was there something happening that we should have seen? Were we, as the sales team, in the wrong? It felt like you were part of something that you shouldn't have been, and nobody offered any answers. At the time, I didn't even know companies could get shut down like that. Learning about regulatory compliance and how important it is and how to run a company ethically became huge priorities for me. I was seeing a new world of direct sales that I never knew existed. What was really shitty about Burn Lounge was who actually had the mud on their face. It was the sales force.

For about a month after the restraining order, conference calls from corporate happened a couple of times a week. They were mostly legal updates—when the next hearing would be, how Burn Lounge was handling it, what lawyers thought might happen. The company made everybody think they'd get through it. But on one of the calls, one of the lawyers made statements about how the FTC had been present in various meetings throughout the course of several months. It became clear Burn Lounge leadership knew what was going on and hadn't been on the up-and-up in communicating with the field. I was not as well versed at that time in business as I am now. I wanted to believe there was light at the end of the tunnel. Hell, at that time I didn't even know what a TRO was. Everything was new to me.

At Burn Lounge, even before the FTC started investigating, I saw how they were sloppy and didn't always do what they said they were going to do. I gave management the benefit of the doubt because they were a startup company and I figured these things happened in the first few years. That's what everybody said, and I was having such a good time, that I wanted to believe everything would be fine. Burn Lounge was the first time I noticed that corporate plays a big role in your success, even if you're a bottom-level salesperson. It isn't just the product. It isn't just the comp plan. I learned how cautious I needed to be if I was to ever do this again and how hard I needed to vet the people controlling the levers at the top. I realized if I was going to put my livelihood into direct selling, being the control freak I am, I needed to connect with the corporate level so I could have more control.

For a few weeks, many of us were hanging on, hoping for an encouraging turn. Then one day the executive team said there would be no more calls. It was over. Burn Lounge was likely shut down for good and if this was your way of making a living, you need to go out and find something else.

I was crushed again. Couldn't I learn lessons and not have it end badly?

When the realization finally hit that Burn Lounge was over, that it was time to pick ourselves up and go do something else, myself and a small group of leaders who had worked closely together at the company began talking with other companies in the direct selling space. We flew out to visit them and we talked with executive teams. We were telling people we wanted to come as a package and had made an informal pact to do that.

I had worked closely with three guys—Jared, Rob and Matt—at Burn Lounge and they were people who I considered friends. They were a part of the initial group that helped get the company started, and I had made them an insane amount of money. As we began to venture out, it became clear as day that whatever was going to happen with this group, this nucleus, these three were not looking out for the team like they portrayed. It quickly became, "What's in the best interest for Jared? What's in the best interest for Rob? What's in the best interest for Matt?" Everyone was trying to out-maneuver one another. We'd hang up the phone on a conference call with a potential landing spot corporate team and Jared would try to call the president and sweeten the deal so it was better for Jared. Or Rob would call the CEO and try to convince the CEO that Rob was the most important piece of the whole deal. There was competitive banter and manipulation. I decided this wasn't the path for me.

That moment was a fork in the road and another life lesson learned. You'll have a lot of people in life that say they're friends with you, that say there is a relationship to be had with you, but the real friends in life are the ones standing there when there's no longer a dollar to be made off you. I was very much a dollar sign to these people and only a pawn in their game. Once I chose to go a different direction, it was only more apparent. The phone calls stopped. The great "relationship" ceased to exist, showing me it had only been about the Benjamins.

Sadly, my head was already spinning with the Burn Lounge disappointment when this second lesson became apparent: seldom in life do you meet people who are truly authentic, who aren't only with you when you are of "value" to them. So when you find those true friends—the ones with no motive—hold on tight.

That was one of many lessons Burn Lounge taught me. Burn Lounge was the second direct sales company I had experienced, so I had something to compare it to. AdvoCare, to me, was a shining example of how to run a business. I thought AdvoCare was the classiest company, the best people, it was managed so well, and the people were so ethical. As successful and fun as Burn Lounge was, I actually saw the opposite of that. I saw Burn Lounge being operated not by the best people, with a sloppy approach to detail. They were terrible at paying their commissions, their customer service was the worst you've ever seen, and they didn't do what they said they were going to do. You never knew if they're lying or telling the truth.

For the first time in my career I learned there were good players and bad players in this space. There were well-managed companies and mismanaged ones. But the real lesson in business is it's that way in every industry. Not just direct sales. So do your homework on all companies and the people owning and running them.

I had no idea where to go or what to do after Burn Lounge, but I had proven to myself that I belonged in this business. I learned that I actually had what it takes to do well and I found my place in the food chain. At AdvoCare I thought I knew my place, and that was at the bottom. I was sure there was something wrong with me. Instead, I learned I actually had what it takes. I wasn't sure what was next for me in direct sales, but I knew this industry was for me.

CHAPTER 7

Life After Burn Lounge: bHIP

There was a lot to think about as Tracy and I headed north on Interstate 65 from Tennessee to Kentucky on a two-and-a-half-hour drive that we both hoped would be a rebound opportunity after the Burn Lounge disaster, which had caused months of angst and disappointment. I found myself at a crossroads as the yellow center lines flew by, creating a blurred singular line pointing directly toward our eagerly anticipated weekend-long meeting. While I felt more confident than ever before in my ability to make the direct sales industry work, and was determined to continue forward, there was an unknown about what the future would hold. I was looking for true partnerships, ones that went beyond dollar signs and focused on building something great. I knew it could be done, but it wasn't quite that simple. I had learned so much but was having trouble believing in others. Even so, I had no choice but to make another call, in search of the next move.

A few days before Tracy and I embarked on this trip, I had contacted a gentleman named Brian, who was also highly successful at Burn Lounge. Brian was based in Louisville and had been at Burn Lounge from the very beginning as one of the first distributors, but he had faded into the shadows toward the end and nobody knew much about him. I knew Brian had made a lot of money at Burn Lounge, maybe even the most of anyone, and as we talked by phone I found that we seemingly had a lot of other things in common, too. Like me, Brian knew all too well about the disappointments and the mismanagement of Burn Lounge, and that's what had ultimately led to his pulling back from the company. The company's poor leadership had been going on for so long that it had stolen Brian's passion. I was in my late 20s but my roughly 10 years in the direct sales industry gave me a lot more knowledge than the typical direct selling distributor. Still, my resume was a bit of a mixed bag at that point. I didn't make much money during my eight years at AdvoCare, but I unknowingly had built a wealth of knowledge that I hadn't quite tapped into yet. On the surface it looked like I had failed at AdvoCare and, from a monetary perspective, I had. My experience at Burn Lounge was the opposite. During my short time there, I had a lot of success and made what people would consider big money in direct sales. I was the one teaching others how to build teams, how to build organizations and how to handle customers. It was a complete paradigm shift at Burn Lounge. But it wasn't like I had a kick-ass resume.

Brian, on the other hand, did. And he was more than willing to tell you about it. Brian was proud to tell me the story of his career and how much money he had made. On our phone call he told me how he'd been a top performer here and a top person there. A little bit of name-dropping, to say the least. "Wow," I thought to myself, "here's a guy that has achieved what I want to achieve and I'm relating to him." I felt a connection with Brian on the phone. Brian was a little bit older than me, well polished and well put together, which made for an instant connection. Having quickly determined it might be a business match, Tracy and I drove 175 miles north from Nashville to Louisville to spend the weekend with Brian.

It didn't take long for me to lock arms with Brian and go on to the next steppingstone in my life. When we got to Louisville, everything seemed like a good fit. Brian was educated, he was well spoken, he had his act together in life. He had a nice house, he had nice cars. Once again, here I was getting starry-eyed with cars! But it wasn't just what I saw. Brian had a great track record, he was very good in direct sales, he was well trained and he knew how to build something. At this moment, in 2007, it felt like the perfect fit. I would later learn one of my greatest life lessons, but that was down the road.

BRIAN AND I SPENT several months discussing what our next play would be and what was important to us. What does the ideal direct sales company look like? We put a lot of thought into that question before we settled on two possible leads in Dallas. The first was one of Brian's childhood friends, Paul Gravette, who was successful in direct sales and was the co-founder of a company called Drink A.C.T. He was someone I definitely wanted to meet. The other lead was a guy named Terry LaCore, who at that time had built Lexxus International into a global company.

Our meeting with Paul at the offices of Drink A.C.T. was short-lived. Paul's pitch was for us to join him at Drink A.C.T., which Brian and I immediately had some hesitation about doing. It was the beginning of the healthy energy drink era and Drink A.C.T. was one of the first products of the canned energy drink movement. But Brian and I had been stung badly by Burn Lounge and not having any corporate control or say with the company had left a bitter taste in our mouths. Paul already had Drink A.C.T. up and running and he couldn't offer any control. He was simply looking for distributors and Brian and I wanted a much larger role. The company was mildly successful, but I deduced very quickly during our trip to the corporate offices that it was a mismanaged company, held together by duct tape and promises. It was easy to see it wasn't a class act like an AdvoCare when I was there, which I continued to judge my opportunities against. When Burn Lounge went down in flames, I told myself I needed to be more mindful of the inner workings of a company. Paul seemed like a great guy during our meeting but there were too many red flags with Drink A.C.T. We shook hands with Paul, thanked him and focused our attention on what Terry might have to offer in our second meeting.

There was no doubt Terry was one of the most successful people I had ever met at that point in my life. Terry had built Lexxus International and taken it from nothing to a company that had achieved $600 million in sales in 30 countries and eventually went public as NHT Global. Terry was the first executive I had met that was not only successful as a distributor, but he had also built a successful global company and made millions of dollars personally. What I liked about Terry was he was very much like me: details matter, being up front with people matters and running a tight ship matters. You don't accidentally grow a company to

$600 million. Terry was more along the lines of running a professional business like an AdvoCare, so a lot of the boxes were checked during our first meeting. Not only did Terry pass the eye test, but Brian and I were going to be a part of the corporate team. We were going to have a founding role and a say in the direction of this new company. Coming out of the Burn Lounge crisis, that was the number one thing Brian and I were seeking. I wanted to have some say on the corporate side in my next step. From the first meeting with Terry, that was exactly what was being offered.

When we flew down to Dallas to meet with Terry, we didn't know his full story. We knew there was something going on with his company, just like he knew there was something going on with Burn Lounge. But we didn't drill each other. We knew we both had some baggage, but we were determined to see if there was a partnership at hand. What we later learned was that during his leadership of Lexxus International and later NHT Global, they ran into an SEC investigation that led the board to terminate his employment. Banished from the company he founded and built, Terry now had what seemed like bottled-up resentment to go build a bigger and better company. But there was nothing about Terry's mannerisms or any red flags during our first meeting that threw us off, and both sides needed each other to take the next step. Terry had the money to back the new company, as well as the software, operations and support team. What Brian and I brought to the table was the sales force. We had the following that could build up the field from the large teams coming out of Burn Lounge. After Burn Lounge went under, I began having regular weekly conference calls with 2,000-4,000 members in the field, letting them know what was going on and what possibilities we were pursuing. There was a nucleus of people that still liked the direct sales industry and knew what happened to Burn Lounge didn't have anything to do with me or Brian. There was still a lot of optimism of, "Let's try to make a win out of this. Let's put something good together and continue carrying the torch." These people were looking to us to find the right home and were waiting on us to see what play we called next.

Brian and I were disgusted and hurt by what had happened with Burn Lounge and were determined to do everything we could to not let it happen again. Who wants to keep starting over in life? It was awful. We agreed to join forces with a common goal: Let's build a generational business and not have to start over again.

We were able to get the company up and running fairly quickly, just six months from that first meeting in Dallas. A lot of that had to do with Terry's experience and his resources. It was just the three of us out of the gate when we met at the Omni, but once things started, we each began calling colleagues and the company picked up steam. Terry wanted to name the company bHIP. I know what you're thinking: That's cool, like "Be Hip." That was Terry's spin. "Everyone wants to be hip in life." We did want to be a new wave of direct sales, so the name stuck. A week or so after we joined forces, we were back at the Omni trying to figure out what the perfect product would be. We began throwing around these cutting-edge, difference-making, concepts.

"What about sublingual strips like a Listerine?" was one idea. The technology was new back then and you could put vitamins and minerals on it.

Instead, the conversation kept coming back to this powdered energy drink. Sure, it might be a great product to have in the portfolio, it might be highly consumed and a great residual for the company. But I remember thinking, "This is no Super Bowl quarterback. How do you build a billion-dollar company on this?"

That was the first red flag I saw at bHIP.

The other red flag came shortly after when Terry invited one of his lifelong best friends, John, to meet with us during one of our meetings at the Omni. Terry thought John could be the perfect president and figurehead of sorts for the company. I had never met John before, and he seemed like a nice guy, but when he showed up to the hotel, he was wearing jeans with holes in them, a fishing shirt and hiking boots. It only got worse. During the meeting, he kicked off the hiking boots and put his feet up on the coffee table, pulled out a bag of McDonald's, and as he was eating this greasy hamburger, he dropped ketchup and mustard on his shirt. I was sitting there freaking out. "No offense to this guy, but this is not a president of a company." I had been around a lot of sharp people from AdvoCare—class acts, people that truly fit the mold of a billion-dollar company. Even as sloppy as Burn Lounge was managed from an operational perspective, those guys were really sharp looking. I was already skittish and nervous because of Burn Lounge and now there was this. I don't remember exactly what I told Brian and Terry, but it was pretty close to, "As good of a person as John may be, if this is the image we're interested in creating, I'm out." John never ended up as bHIP's president and I decided to continue on as we built up the sales force.

The problem? There was nothing novel about bHIP. As I had come through all these companies before, they stood out. AdvoCare was prestigious, classy and organized. Burn Lounge wasn't the classiest or most ethical, but they had an incredible, novel business model. It was so sexy, fun and glamorous. Then there was bHIP, which was anything but hip. We were well run and ethical, we did things the right way because Terry had done it before, but there was nothing unique about bHIP. All we had was a little energy powder packet. That was it—one product. There was nothing revolutionary about the product, nothing innovative about the company. I was pulling my hair out, "Guys, this won't fly. We're in a very competitive space. This isn't going to get the job done." A few months earlier I was talking about the digital music movement and big-name celebrity investors and now we were talking about an energy powder that's the cornerstone of a billion-dollar business? It was not great marketing and nowhere near an innovative business model. Out of all the options we had discussed, this was almost a knock-off product similar to what Paul had with Drink A.C.T. Drink A.C.T. had a packet, we had a packet and AdvoCare had one called Spark.

Although Brian and I had done really well in Burn Lounge, we didn't have the money Terry had. When we joined forces, one of the things Terry was passionate about was that he was happy to help put the company together, to help create a forever home, but he was going to be the owner. That was how things were going to roll. bHIP was my first entry into the corporate side of the fence and my first time behind the curtain, so I wasn't in a position to demand that I have ownership. Nor did I have a ton of capital sitting around to make it happen. At the end of the day, Terry made the decisions. As much as I knew Terry ran a tight ship and would operate the company well, I wasn't terribly optimistic about the success the business model would have.

When we launched bHIP, I still had a feeling I was going to have a lot of people join the company. I had over 20,000 people in my Burn Lounge business and during my conference calls leading up to bHIP, there was definitely a synergy. When Burn Lounge ended, there was a lot that happened. There were people that threw in the towel completely, so distraught they would never touch direct sales again. But there was a large group of people that were ready for the next big thing. In the final days of Burn Lounge, the vice president told me, "You never knew this, but your team was the fastest growing team in the entire company. A lot of the other parts of the company had stopped growing and your team was really the only growing part of the company." He was essentially telling me, "You *were* Burn Lounge in these final months. You and your team *were* the company." In the lead-up to bHIP there was an excitement that Jason and the team had found something that was going to be big. Everybody wanted to know about it first and jump on it. There was still that optimism coming out of Burn Lounge. When it was revealed what the decision was—this company with a cool name and an experienced owner—I sensed excitement. Once people finally found out what the product actually was, we lost a lot of people and that excitement. When the dust finally settled, I got around 4,000 people out of the gate for bHIP's launch. I felt like even some of the people I did get to join forces only agreed to take a leap of faith because of my credibility with them, not their energy for the product.

Terry was a very smart businessman and a great numbers guy, and although I liked him and his management style, once bHIP was in full swing, other things started coming out of the closet. Terry and his team were great at operations, shipped product perfectly, paid commissions on time and handled customer service to a T. But they didn't have the talent or skillset from a marketing or branding perspective.

What are we going to do next? What was our next product going to be? There was nothing. We were just going to stick with this one energy powder because the one-product philosophy was easy to scale internationally. There was no hipness, no novel approach to the product line. It was insanely hard to be attractive to the end consumer, the soccer mom or your golf buddy. The only people bHIP related to was some network marketing junkie who had done this before and thought it would be really awesome if he or she could scale that quickly into all these countries. The company was on a downhill slope as soon as it got going. I started thinking, "Whoa, we're not on the same page." It became clear that Terry was making many of his moves to get back at his former company that had forced him out. We later found out that NHT Global's publicly traded NASDAQ ticker was: BHIP.

The name bHIP was merely a slap in NHT's face.

At that time of my life, my business skillset and awareness were beginning to pick up a lot of steam. I was learning and getting better every day. From the executive side to the corporate side to the distributor side, not only was I able to start picking these things up, I was also able to start putting a business plan together on why companies were succeeding and failing in this space. With bHIP, I learned a valuable lesson that would inform my future in this industry.

I've seen direct selling companies formed two ways: The bulk of direct selling companies are started as bHIP was, with some experienced guys who get together, start a company and then try to come up with a product. The other way direct selling companies start is when people get behind a product. "Look at this new product that we just got our hands on. Oh, my. This is such a big game-changer. We need to launch a company around this." I see direct selling companies begin both ways and the ones that succeed most are focused on a product. Those are the companies that are the most authentic, the most passionate and innovative. That's what resonates best with the consumer. Not, "Let's start a company. Then, let's go get a product." I still believe that's why bHIP ended up never amounting to much. It was just another company with nothing novel other than this very experienced person owning it. That ended up becoming the story of the company. When we were in motion and bHIP was fully in business, the pitch, the story, ended up being about Terry and about how his previous company went to 30 countries. That doesn't resonate with the everyday person. They don't care if your company can go into 30 countries, or how big it can grow.

Nobody really understands what direct selling is to begin with, and when you don't have a product that's really exciting or different to the end consumer you become a "direct selling junkie company." Always remember, people relate to products, not opportunities.

What I wanted to do in direct sales, and what I had seen with AdvoCare and Burn Lounge, were two companies that related to people that didn't have anything to do with direct selling. They found the product appealing from a consumer perspective and therefore the business made sense. It was completely opposite with bHIP, which became one of the biggest learning experiences I've ever had in the direct selling space. I learned how *not* to do it.

I see executives and entrepreneurs from other sectors and other industries come into this realm and they think they're going to launch a company and will make billions of dollars in sales and they fall on their face every time because they don't know or understand the culture.

Direct sales is about building a volunteer army. The sales force doesn't have to do anything, they don't have to work for you, they don't have to like your product. I've seen direct sales companies work both ways, but I believe the best way is when a true innovative product and idea comes about and because of that it makes sense to launch a company. A lot of these companies run around talking about the opportunity and it runs everybody off. Who in the world wakes up in the morning wanting to join a company with no real product? That doesn't relate to people. When you sell a product that people get passionate about, there's meaning behind the product and it makes sense to people when you later bring up potentially selling the product. Light bulbs go off because they have conviction and passion about the product. It's not just a money game. That was bHIP's biggest challenge and ultimately its biggest roadblock. Even when you saw bHIP continue to mature as the months and years went on, it never got any fancier or more innovative. It was this very old school network marketing approach. It was only attractive to industry professionals that had been in the business forever and had huge followings and international markets. They liked Terry and bHIP because Terry had operated previously in Asia. There was nothing attractive to the average American or Canadian or anybody in North America.

One of my biggest goals in direct selling became to build a company that relates to the average person. I began to look at companies who I felt did it the right way like Mary Kay, Avon or NuSkin. I look at companies that have been in business for 20 to 30 years and that's what I eventually created Le-Vel to be. I don't have to be the biggest. Sure, I want to win, I want my company to be the best out there. But my ultimate goal is to build the absolute best product line I can.

When you really believe in something, you're willing to keep going and going and going. At AdvoCare, I believed in who they were at that time and what they did, I believed in the product, I believed in the management, I believed in the company and it carried me through even when I wasn't finding success. With bHIP, I lost complete belief. I didn't believe in the product and I didn't believe in where the company was going. There wasn't any passion, there wasn't any conviction.

Terry and Brian got frustrated, and Brian shared some of my concerns. What we talked about in the early days—what we could do and what we could be—quickly disappeared and here we were stuck with this subpar product, awful marketing and no desire to be anything more. That was so far from who I was and what type of company I wanted to be associated with. I traveled all over the United States and lived on the road. I went where my volume and my team was located. It wasn't attractive or relatable to the everyday person. I didn't believe in the company, I didn't believe in where it was going, and therefore I needed to cut my losses and start over yet again.

It wouldn't be the last time I'd have to start over in my career, but here I was having to start from scratch. Again. What do I do next in this direct selling space?

CHAPTER 8

Relationship Lessons & Leading ABG

As I prepared to start over once again in direct sales, I didn't lack confidence about what I could build. Things were starting to make sense to me, and I was beginning to dissect the mistakes I had encountered with previous companies. Sure, I was sick of having to go back to the beginning over and over, and I so badly wanted something to stick. But while I had to grapple with all the lessons I was learning in this industry, what kept me moving forward was what I could *feel* around me. When I finally decided bHIP wasn't for me, I made the rounds to inform people I had networked with of my decision. I wasn't downing or bashing bHIP, I was simply explaining that my heart wasn't there and I was going to look at something else. Probably 85 percent told me they felt similarly, that they too weren't exactly thrilled with the company's direction. "Let us know what we're doing next," some of them told me. It was almost: "OK, coach, you call the play." There were some people who were just done with direct sales, and I lost some people and some credibility. But the real movers and shakers, the people that really moved the needle on my team, I captured a lot of them. I felt so inspired. It felt like a testament to me as a leader that these people thought of me as a person, over and above the semi-failed bHIP energy movement.

Backed by a large support group, myself and some of the top leaders from my bHIP team started making calls in search of the next opportunity. One of my leaders came to me with an interesting lead: "There are some very successful business guys out of Tampa, Fla., that have never owned a direct sales company, but they are very familiar with the model and they're looking for the right guy to be the president of a new company." Every opportunity at this point was worth vetting, and the opportunity to lead a company intrigued me. So I got on the phone with this lead, John Buschel, a proclaimed self-made millionaire, and his business partner, an ex-professional wrestler named Brian "The Bear" Klinge, in hopes of starting this new direct sales company. John was the figurehead of the partnership and explained that he had started several telecommunication companies that ran the infrastructure and operations for a number of call centers that sold various products. John proclaimed he had made millions doing this and had come across a cool new concept for a direct selling company. But John and The Bear had no experience in the direct selling space, so his pitch was that they would provide the capital, but they needed someone to provide the expertise and leadership on the front end.

When I left bHIP, I hadn't conveyed my reasons to anyone except Brian, who had been with me since the beginning of bHIP. He seemed to be just as frustrated with the company's lack of success and innovation. On my way out, Brian made it clear he wanted to follow me wherever I ended up. "I'm with you," he told me. "Let's do it together." Brian's fear was that he didn't have a lot of horses in his barn. Even though bHIP wasn't a successful company, I had been one of the main leaders of the field and had one of the biggest teams. I think Brian knew he needed to stay with me to leverage that. I just didn't know he was trying to leverage me to the extent he was. I saw Brian's character flaws in my year and a half at bHIP, but he hadn't totally exposed himself as a bad apple. When I brought Brian into the discussion with John and The Bear, everything appeared to be moving in the right direction. John was ready to take the next step. "You guys sound great," he told us. "Let's meet face to face." They sent us plane tickets, and bHIP Brian was set to fly down to Tampa from Louisville while I readied for my trip from Dallas. This was when bHIP Brian finally revealed himself to the ultimate extent. I had made the decision to bring Brian into the fold for this possible opportunity, but I was on my last straw with him after I saw how he tried to manipulate people at bHIP and made attempts to divide me and Terry by telling lies about me. The night before we were set to fly to Tampa to meet with John and The Bear, Brian called me to ask what I was planning to wear. "These guys told me they're very down to earth and they're not going to be in suits, and I think we need to respect that," he said. "I'm going to wear jeans and a button-down shirt untucked." I agreed, and the next morning I got dressed in business casual clothes and headed to the airport. Thank the Lord my flight got canceled and I couldn't make the meeting. I called John in a panic. "John, this is not who I am. You tell me to be somewhere, I'm going to be there. I'm a man of my word," I told him. "They can't get me to Tampa." Later that day, after he and The Bear had met with Brian, John called me. "Brian is not our guy, we're sending him back home. We still want to meet with you, we like how you say what you say. Brian is just not our guy," he said. "By the way, please come dressed comfortable. Brian wore this three-piece bullshit suit with a tie and didn't speak very highly of you." I couldn't believe it. That's how manipulating Brian was. He had tried to get me to wear something that would make me look like the inferior talent in the room. When I confronted Brian, he gave me a bullshit answer. "I decided dressing to impress was the better approach," he said. The way he said it, he was almost throwing it in my face. From that moment on I never returned a phone call from Brian. He blew my phone up for weeks like a scorned girlfriend that calls 15 times a day and sends texts. I never talked to him again.

I did learn a valuable lesson about leadership from Brian. I don't see Brian as a bad guy, but he was a very insecure person. I should have seen through it earlier. I remember when I first met Brian he would never call me. He would text me 50 times a day and most of them were two words: "Call me." For the first several months I'd pick up the phone and call him, but it started to get old. I wasn't his pager. Why was he always asking me to call him? One day he kept sending me text messages: "Call me," "Call me," "Call me." I let the day go by without calling him, and he finally broke down and phoned me. Eventually, I kept pressing him on why he was always asking me to call him. Why didn't he ever just call me? "Look, I'll tell you something," he said. "You always want to remain in control with people and doing things like telling people to call you is a psychological way to remain in control." Who thinks that way? I wasn't trying to control people; I was trying to be a leader and a successful businessperson. Brian definitely taught me how *not* to be a leader in life. What I've learned is that the best leaders want to build up stronger leaders around them. If you think about the strongest CEOs out there, and the right way to build a company, you build up leaders stronger and bigger and better than yourself. That's Leadership 101. In direct sales, you build up a volunteer army because people believe in who you are and what you are and they *choose* to follow you. Brian just wanted to keep everybody beneath him, and I couldn't get where I wanted to go with him dragging me down.

I DID EVENTUALLY MAKE it down to Tampa and met with John and The Bear. John was about 250 pounds and looked like a mobster and Brian was indeed a bear. They didn't look anything like the leaders of a company, and they recognized it. "We don't want to be the face of the company," John told me. "Direct sales is not our background. That's why we're partnering with a guy like you. You be the face. You run the company. You call the shots. We will be the financing behind it." Although I knew up front that these were not the classiest guys, I was in a very desperate situation and everything seemed great. This was going to be my first chance to be the president of a company, and while it didn't look or feel the best, it seemed like a great opportunity to take a piece of clay and mold a company in my vision. I determined that I shouldn't judge the book by its total cover. Plus, as I had learned at bHIP, an innovative product was key, and these two guys had seemingly come across something game changing.

While running his call centers, John had a company come to him that had spent 18 months putting together a website where you paid for a monthly membership and got access to a portal where you entered your ZIP code and got discounts to everything you could imagine. There were thousands of restaurants, businesses, gas stations, hotels and rental cars. The list went on and on and on. Everything that you spend money on daily, you could find a way to save in this portal. It really added up to substantial savings. When I first met John and The Bear, the whole idea sounded gimmicky. These things always seemed to be smoke and mirrors that made it seem like you could save money. But, as I began to play around with the portal, I saw it was legit. There was 20 percent off at Chili's here and 30 percent cash back there. I could see this was going to work right away because it made sense to the end consumer. I immediately started putting this business plan together: "If you're going to spend money, get cash back on the money you're already spending." It was no different than something like a credit card. If you're going to use one, why not get 2 percent cash back on money you're going to spend anyway? The product was brilliant.

About two weeks later, after I had put together this incredible business plan and we settled on the name Acquire Benefits Group, it was go-time. We were ready to take a step toward launching the company, and John and Brian invited me back to Tampa to move forward with the process. It was a Friday night and the two of them told me they wanted to take me to a nice dinner. "I really like a good steak and a martini," I told them. "We know the best place in Tampa," they said, "People fly in to go eat at this steakhouse." After meeting all day we made our way to the steakhouse. When we pulled into the parking lot it definitely fit the bill. There were Bentleys and Lamborghinis. When we walked in the building, there were all these beautiful women, and not one of them had a top on. It was a legitimate, high-end steakhouse, but none of the girls wore tops. I still remember sitting down to start on appetizers and The Bear had a well-breasted blonde sitting on his knee. As he was eating his shrimp cocktail, he accidentally dropped cocktail sauce on her breast. "Oh my gosh," I thought, "who did I just get in business with? This is a nightmare. Why can't I find normal, good people?"

John and The Bear might have been sleazy, but it wasn't like they were going to be the face of the company. The product was perfect, and I was certain the launch was going to be a hit. Acquire Benefits Group was my baby. It was everything I wanted to do, done how I wanted to do it. I was the maestro. Everything was mine, there was no one there to say, "No, we don't want to do that," or "We don't want to spend money there." I had a blank canvas to build the company, and that's what I did. I built the concept, built the compensation plan and built the marketing plan. And it was one of the most successful pre-launches direct sales has ever seen.

Leading up to the launch, we were doing conference calls to talk about the company, and we'd get anywhere from 10,000 to 20,000 people on calls, which crashed and overloaded the system. Eventually, we had to have conference call companies tag team and work together to bridge phone lines. During the two-week pre-launch, we pre-registered 25,000 people for the product. The company hadn't even launched yet and I was getting applauded everywhere. Everyone was in awe at how well the company was put together. It was cheers all the way around, and it was looking as cool and as sexy and as fun as Burn Lounge had been. The timing made sense, the story made sense and it was a product anybody could find value in regardless of if they liked direct sales or not. It just made sense. It was an absolute rocket ship from the beginning.

In the days leading up to the launch, I did everything I could to make sure we were ready. John and Brian were not business or direct sales savvy at all, and I remember calling Brian a few days before launch. "Look," I said, "our merchant provider needs to be ready. We've got 25,000 people signed up in the system. When we flip the switch here, we're going to generate millions of dollars at once. We need the merchant processor to be ready to rock, because this thing's gonna hum." Brian assured me everything was ready with the merchant credit card processor. "I'm on it. The guy is a personal friend of mine. We've been friends forever. He's given us a thumbs up," Brian said. I wasn't talking to the credit card company myself, but I took Brian's word for it. I had double, triple, quadruple checked with him and was told we were a go each time.

When we finally flipped the switch—Boom!—we processed pre-enrollment registrations and ABG was the hottest thing known to mankind in direct sales. We generated $1.8 million in the first 24 hours in business. Then the shit hit the fan. The next day, the credit card company froze our funds, telling us their compliance department had audited the company and, in their policies and procedures, it stated they didn't allow direct sales companies. And even if they did, they said, our account had a $300,000 processing limit. Here we were, the greatest company pre-launching in America at that time, everything was golden, and in one day our funds were frozen. We immediately got on calls with attorneys and the merchant processing company's compliance department, but they dug their heels in. They said they didn't know who ABG was, if it was going to be in business in 30 days or not and that it was too risky to release the money. I got a crash course and PhD in credit card processing in one day and saw firsthand how it can be an ultimate death blow if not executed properly. It turned out that Brian's friend was only a sales guy, he wasn't upper management.

What they were really scared of were possible chargebacks. For example, if you processed $300,000 right now in orders and the merchant processor deposited the money in your business bank account two days later and you distributed that as commissions, the money is gone. Let's say ABG did turn out to be a scam, the product never shipped and these 25,000 customers called their bank to get their money back. When the bank starts issuing chargebacks, if the company doesn't have the money, the credit card processing company is left holding the bag. There is a lot of risk for these merchant processing companies and they are skittish about the whole thing (especially for startups). What most banks and credit card companies do is allow you to put money down in a reserve account in the event things go wrong. If Brian would have set up the merchant account the way it was supposed to be and backed it financially to eliminate the risk, ABG would have been off and running. It was the most unfortunate thing, because the credit card processing company seized the $1.8 million we had generated. Plus, they didn't even allow direct sales companies in the first place! Everything about the setup with the credit card processing company was wrong and it was the demise, almost immediately, of Acquire Benefits Group. We had just generated all these sales, which triggered commissions to the field and now we couldn't pay them. We fought with the processing company and every day this went on—Day 2, Day 3, Day 4—was absolutely killing us.

We slowly limped along after the freeze. John and Brian didn't think the mishap was that big of a deal. I was freaking out going, "Oh shit, this is over before it's even starting. This is horrible." They thought it was no big deal, that we'd just go get the right merchant processor and keep going. We did end up getting another credit card processing company, but by then the buzz, the passion, was gone. That special synergy of ABG being the next big company was absolutely destroyed when the company was unable to process credit cards or pay commissions. The field was distraught. Everybody was quitting. John and Brian told me they were out of money. They were supposed to be so well off, with a couple million dollars to throw at this startup, and now they were telling me they had run dry. It was a house of cards that was destroyed instantly. What's so fickle about the direct sales space is people are almost expecting you to fail because you're a startup and all these companies start and they go and then they vanish. Before you can ever get going, people are already nervous, and if you give them anything—you don't ship your product on time, you don't handle customer service on time or you don't pay commissions—if it isn't flawless, you're almost validating their fear in the back of their mind that this thing is not going to last or that this is a flash in the pan. When we had to come clean with everybody in the field and tell them about the colossal issue on our hands, it was so unfortunate. As quickly as ABG launched it fizzled—in about two weeks, the company was gone because Brian and John didn't have $1.8 million to continue to float the company and pay the commissions. It was an absolute nightmare. And as the leader of this whole operation, the mud was on *my* face.

Up until this point in my life, I had not been an emotional person. I'm very emotional in terms of being a dreamer and doer and fired up about what I want to do in life. But I'd never been someone to feel stress or worry. For whatever reason, in tough times I was always cool as a cucumber. Even when I moved to Nashville and was living off of a credit card, eating canned tuna, could barely pay bills and was broke, it never bothered me. I never had stress or anxiety. I just kept going. When everything happened with Acquire Benefits Group, it was the first time in my life where I experienced emotions like anxiety, panic and stress. It wasn't just that I had mud on my face; it was that I knew how devastating these moments were for other people. Not long before, I had seen how Burn Lounge's corporate leadership had crushed people's hopes and dreams. Now here I was leading the charge. These were my people, my following, my team that I had brought to the table. And now it was all gone. Everybody was saying, "Jason, what the hell happened? Are you kidding me? This isn't you." I was still trying to be the president of the company, but I was incredibly mad at John and Brian. I had asked Brian 300 times if we were good with the merchant processor, if they were comfortable handling the large volume. We went over it again and again. As the leader, I was trying not to point my finger, but I was beginning to speak out of both sides of my mouth.

For a few weeks I flew to meet with the small group of people who were still willing to make ABG go. During one of the meetings at a hotel, I met this man who, for a lack of a better description, was a big, Italian, mob-looking guy. After the meeting he asked to have a word with me in private, where he proceeded to tell me John and The Bear weren't wealthy, and in fact didn't have any money or a pot to piss in, that they had borrowed $250,000 from a lady named Marcy. Marcy and her husband had owned a butcher shop for a lifetime and out of the excitement of what this could be, they loaned John and Brian $250,000 to get ABG started. This guy told me he was skeptical of how this whole thing went down and thought there might be fraud involved. He said John's story of the telecommunications company was true, but the piece I didn't know was that his business was raided by the FBI and SEC for fraud. It went from bad to worse to so dirty and icky. After we left the hotel that night, the guy would call once a week for a period of time. Other people in the company that knew more about him told me that, as nice as the guy was, he had ties to the mob and that I should keep my distance from him. When everything I thought I knew about John and Brian proved to be false, I focused on sorting through the crap. It was time for me to, once again, move down the road.

There were a lot of lessons that came from Acquire Benefits Group. At bHIP I had learned that without an innovative product it's hard to have success in direct sales. At ABG, I found out that it's definitely still a people business, even if the product is game-changing. You can have great people and great credibility, but if the product is shitty, the company isn't going to be any good. On the other hand, if you have an incredible product with really sloppy management and bad people, you can end up in the same place. The sad thing was, I chose two bad partners. It wasn't like I was fooled. I saw early on that these probably weren't the best people to be in business with, but this was my shot to be president of a company. Looking back, I think about that night at the steakhouse. I guess when you see cocktail sauce on a topless woman's breast, it is probably a red flag!

But my gut had told me to go for it. I didn't have a lot of options coming into ABG and I didn't necessarily have a winning resume either. Sure, I did really well at Burn Lounge, but that got shut down. I had some great behind-the-curtain experience with bHIP, but I had left that, too. So it wasn't like I could go to a first class, $100 million direct sales company and say, "Hey, I want to be your president." John and Brian saw me as the best they could get and, while I knew there was risk and all the boxes weren't checked, I also felt I needed to go for this. Yes, it didn't look completely right, there were some oddities and red flags, but

I thought it could be a good opportunity for me. John and Brian weren't the greatest people, but I can unequivocally say they had no desire for the company to fail, they just weren't great business people.

While Acquire Benefits Group ended up being a massive failure and a big black eye for me personally, it was where I started sharpening my sword as a C-level executive. It may have been short-lived, but we were the hottest startup company in the entire country, and there was no doubt it could have worked. That doesn't happen by accident. When direct sales companies start, it takes them awhile to get going. We pre-registered 25,000 people in two weeks and did nearly $2 million the very first day. Who knows what could have been? We might have been a $75 million company in Year 1. ABG was a disaster, but it's where I began to spread my wings as an executive and learn how to build a business and marketing plan and put it all into motion. That's when I saw for the first time that I could do *everything* myself. I found out at Burn Lounge that I could succeed, but now I saw that I was not only talented, I was really freaking good in this area. This was my first day as the president of the company, as a C-level executive, and I was starting to learn where I fit in the food chain of this industry. I wasn't at the bottom. I was a lion.

I felt terrible for people like Marcy and all the members of the field who I had let down. We did a lot of emergency company update calls and luckily The Bear took complete ownership of his merchant processing mistake and took the axe without me having to throw it. Not that I would have. Before the collapse, ABG was a 10 out of 10, and ironically my following grew because a lot of people had come to learn of me and who I was through the company. It certainly wasn't a good thing that happened, but again I had a ton of people looking at me going, "Jason, what's next? What do we do now?"

It was around this time that my old friend, Wes, had reached out and apologized about how AdvoCare ended. When ABG went down, I told him about what had happened and talked about the pressure I felt. "I've got to go find a home for these people," I told him. "There's all these people that are now looking at me going, 'Jason, what's next? Let's go do something.'" He told me it sounded like a book he was reading called *Tribes*. I immediately got the book and start reading it. "We want you to lead us," it read. I was ready to start over again. Yes, I had mud on my face, but I still had this large group looking to me.

CHAPTER 9

LifeCore Global

n the few weeks after the Acquire Benefits Group fiasco, it was a flat-out rampage. There was an urgency to find the next home for the thousands of followers who had been in the field, and I could feel the pressure. You have to move fast in times like these because there are plenty of others who would love to scoop up your people to build their own sales force. Knowing time was of the essence, I reached out to my top 20 or so leaders: We needed to find something and fast. We needed to explore all possibilities and consider all options, whether it was to start a new company or join an existing one. My leaders reached out to owners, executives, anybody they knew in the direct sales industry, while I started calling the names in my Rolodex. We had one huge selling point in our search: There's a large group of people assembled, and we're looking for a home.

That was the silver lining in all of this and why my spirits weren't totally crushed when ABG went under. Yes, I was pissed that what should have been a huge success turned into a dud, but I was emboldened by this massive group ready to follow me and create *the next big thing* in direct sales. I could send out an email to my main leaders about a team update call and later that day there would be 5,000 people on a call. That's the funny thing about this business. You're coming out of what was perceived to be a colossal failure and it's almost like there's this high that people get from the thought of beginning something new. There's wonderment in the idea of, "What if this goes to a billion dollars and I'm in at the beginning?" As bad as what we had just went through at ABG, when we started talking there was a positive outlook on the next step in the journey. "OK, that hurt and that happened, but now I'm back onto this high of this new startup and getting in the game with all this synergy." What I've come to learn is that moment is when the company is the sexiest, because you get to call people about something that's just taking off. It's kind of like getting the inside scoop on a stock that's going to be really huge. Nobody knows about it yet and you're the first to find out. So in those few weeks, as we scrambled to find a new home, this incredible energy started building. People wanted to know, and they wanted to know first.

For several weeks I fielded call after call, talking to companies and getting introduced to people through my network of leaders. Amidst all these calls I reconnected with Terry, who probably had a bitter taste in his mouth because when I had left bHIP a bunch of people had followed me. But Terry was a businessman at heart, and I think he saw me calling as an opportunity to potentially make money. Terry had seen from the sidelines how successful ABG had been at the start. It was like, "You guys were killing it. Yeah, you tripped up and fell on your face but, man, that thing was hot." He had seen me perform at a much higher caliber than I had at bHIP because all those things I had told him matter—marketing, look and feel, having sex appeal and a unique product—were at the core of ABG. "What do you want to do?" Terry asked when we met. I explained we were exploring all avenues and had found an investor who was willing to be a partner and had $1 million capital to bring to the table. "There's someone I want you to meet," he told me. Terry and I have had our differences, but I was open to exploring ideas. Terry said this guy, Michael Lightfoot, was retired in the industry but he had hired him years back, and he was a great guy, a good family man and might be an experienced partner that I could put something together with. When I met Michael, he was everything Terry built him up to be. He had built a health and nutrition company, Kaire, into a $100 million business, which was extremely successful at the time. At that point in my life, there were very few people I had actually physically met who could say they had started and owned a company to that level. I immediately hit it off with Michael. I was fairly young in 2009, and here was this gray-haired part of the team, who anchored a duo for long-term validation. I had developed great leadership abilities, was being talked about and had a great following, but I never had this anchor, this resume that said, "This guy has done $100 million in business." Michael really filled those gaps. He said he had the capital and the resources to run the operations and customer support for a new startup. Better yet, Michael told me I could control the messaging and help build out an innovative product line. Finally, it seemed, I had found both a unique product *and* a good partner.

Michael had started Kaire in the 1980s and had built his success primarily by selling an antioxidant known as Pycnogenol, which is a medicinal antioxidant from tree bark. There had been a number of studies showing the anti-aging and memory benefits, and Kaire made a substantial number of sales with the product. Michael had sold the business after it had run its course, but he acquired it again not long before we connected. The people who had purchased the company called one day and asked if he wanted it back. They were looking to get it off their books, and Michael bought it for pennies on the dollar. He wasn't really interested in the company, but he had the company's assets along with the experience and resources to build something new. What made Michael so eye-catching to me was that Kaire's success wasn't a flash in the pan. It wasn't a Burn Lounge; it was a company that had been in business for decades and had generated a lot of money. After crashing and burning so many times and after starting over again and again, all I wanted was stability. I was on the search for a long-term play, something where I could stay, put in the work and hang my hat and it would last forever. That's all I wanted.

I WAS RELIEVED WHEN MICHAEL and his wife, Linda, walked into the hotel room where myself and 50 others had gathered so I could introduce them to my new partners and our new business. Michael entered the room in a nice suit and Linda wore a pink shirt with business pants. They perfectly fit the role of what people want to see in a successful company. I was so thankful, because John and The Bear had been the total opposite. And although my following was as big as ever, there was nervousness in the group after some of the recent bumps in the road at bHIP and ABG. I felt an immense pressure that I had to make the right decision this time—the right move, with the right people. That first meeting was perfect, and everything about our new company, LifeCore Global, felt perfect, too.

Michael and I set out to create a brand-new company. Sure, there were some resources and assets to pull from Kaire, but that was icing on the cake. Kaire was more about validation for who Michael was and what he had done right. With LifeCore Global, we took Pycnogenol, the key ingredient from Kaire's star product, and sourced a new line of tree bark from New Zealand, called Enzogenol, which had about five times the antioxidant and anti-aging capabilities of Pycnogenol. Michael had already been testing Enzogenol before we met, so not only did we have a great product, but we also had years of clinical studies and data to back up everything we wanted to say about our tree bark product. The gel capsule was perfect, and we had the clinical studies to prove it. Michael and his team had eight, double-blind, placebo-controlled studies and kicked off the results to a statistician, who provided us with a document concluding that the product would, unequivocally, for every person that took it, provide all these great results within two weeks. We had a grand PDF that showed unequivocal, clinically-backed improvement in cognitive support, eyesight and other improvements and we were thinking we were getting ready to go crush a home run with all that data and science. The company operated smoothly: we shipped products right, we paid commissions right, customer service was right and the marketing was sexy. Everything I knew needed to be there was there.

Then nothing really happened. We eventually got LifeCore Global up to a few hundred thousand in sales a month, which was enough to pay bills and keep the lights on. But it wasn't a smashing success.

That's when I learned a very important lesson about clinical studies and the craziest thing about marketing. The more facts and the more data you give people, the less they actually believe it. It was the craziest thing I had ever seen. I could give someone a PDF that showed, unequivocally, here are the numbers and the numbers don't lie. This is what the product will do for you. We had eight studies from eight universities! Yet the more information I gave people, the more skeptical they were. Instead of saying, "I'm in, here's my credit card," they just started asking more and more questions, wanted to review the studies themselves and wanted to go take the study to their smart doctor friend down the road. It was a damn shame, because Michael and Linda were the perfect partners, and all the boxes were checked. For the life of us, we could not get people to buy this product. There had been various reasons these other ships had gone down. I've told you about Burn Lounge and bHIP and ABG. They all had challenges and crystal-clear reasons they weren't successful, but none of that fit LifeCore Global. Everything should have resulted in a winning company, except for that one valuable lesson. I learned how harmful marketing with scientific studies and all that research can be. You think it's going to help validate your product and generate all these sales, but it does the complete opposite.

The best of the less-is-more examples is Apple. They could go on and on each fall about all the upgrades and the changes they've made to the latest iPhone. They could tell you why the camera is better, how the processing is faster, what the team did in China to get it to the United States. They could give you all this technical jargon, but instead they give you a little paragraph and a cool video and everybody stands in line for hours to buy a phone. The less you say, the less data you give, the more people actually buy. If you look at the world's largest consumer products today, they all have that one thing in common. Mary Kay is one of the largest cosmetic companies on the entire planet. Why is it successful? Is it because they have shown their product is the best with science and data? It's because they built a positive culture of word of mouth and personal, testimonial-driven sales. If you look at any consumer-based brand out there today, that's the catch-22. Everybody thinks people want all this information, but it's not what builds billion-dollar brands. The biggest companies are driven off personal testimony, passion and peer-to-peer consumer excitement. Emotion and personal conviction to a product, to a company, is what gets people to buy, not data and science.

In my company today, Le-Vel, I have a plethora of efficacy and safety studies. Because it's our fiduciary duty to do that. My mom was my first customer at Le-Vel, and my wife was my second, so if my company produces something, I want it to be the safest and most effective. However, I don't believe in marketing with data that overwhelms because of the damage it did and the uphill challenge it created at LifeCore Global. Instead, I use excitement, stories and a less-is-more approach, and it's made all the difference.

The second aspect I learned at LifeCore Global is how important having a high-impact product is. There was no denying that LifeCore had a product that produced results, but they weren't always immediate or evident. We live in a microwave society: people want to see and feel results *now*. LifeCore Global was an anti-aging product where you wouldn't necessarily feel it. It wasn't like AdvoCare, where you took an energy-based product and 15 minutes later you felt it and were bouncing off the walls, or a weight loss product that you took and saw results in seven days. I learned that if I was going to be wildly successful in this direct selling space, I needed to do it with high-impact products where people could feel and see results. As great of a company as LifeCore Global was, as perfect as the management team was and as solid as our science was, you saw an almost lackadaisical, disinterested attitude from the consumer because they wanted energy, excitement, and passion about the product and instant gratification. Not studies and data with no exciting results.

We kept our heads down at LifeCore Global despite the unexciting results. We eventually launched a skincare line and tried to diversify the brand. One of the biggest challenges came when, out of nowhere, we got an e-mail from an attorney representing a dental supply company, LifeCore, which didn't want its brand confused with ours. Our lawyers thought we could ultimately win the dispute, but LifeCore, the dental supply company, was a large company and our lawyers figured we could easily spend $1 million fighting for the name. We decided to change our name to LifeFX Global.

The frustration started to kick in between myself, Michael and Linda, and I became adamant that in order to be successful we needed to have impact products for the younger, hipper and cooler generation. The anti-aging, memory-enhancing tree bark product wasn't appealing to the 38-year-old mother who wants to look better, feel better and have more energy. When I returned from an August vacation on an Alaskan cruise, I received a letter from Michael and Linda about the future of the company. They basically explained that they wanted to part ways. It was obvious where things were heading. We already had discussions before my trip about shutting the company down or letting people go. I understood and wasn't taken back. It wasn't as if I had a lot of passion or belief any longer, and if I don't believe in something it is hard for me to continue. They knew I gave it a go and I knew it wasn't their fault. It was unfortunate. We shook hands and we moved on.

I had been losing people daily during my time at LifeCore/LifeFX Global. People were jumping ship left and right. It wasn't interesting or fun, and we couldn't get any customers or sales or momentum. When the Lightfoots and I shook hands and parted ways, I didn't have a lot of following left. When Burn Lounge ended, I had thousands of people at any given time that I could get on a phone call. They all wanted to hear about my next move, my next decision, where I was going to go and what I was going to do. After ABG ended, as sad as it was, my following was as big as ever. LifeCore/LifeFX Global was totally different. It had been great people, a great company and a great product, but the sales and momentum were horrible. It was almost seen as the worst notch on my resume because all these people had followed me there and, yes, it was well-run, but the feeling from leaders was, "Dude, this is a Ford truck. We want to be in a Ferrari." When I left LifeCore/LifeFX Global, I had the smallest following that I had ever had since beginning in the direct sales industry. No one was really interested.

Truth be told, I should have pulled the plug on LifeCore/LifeFX much earlier, but I was making a decent salary and I was so tired of starting over and over. I knew the company wasn't destined for long-term success, but I was getting paid and went down with the ship. The positive of LifeCore/LifeFX Global was seeing the corporate structure hum and work the way it's supposed to. Looking back, I learned valuable lessons that acted as crucial steppingstones in my career. I really wanted to succeed. I really wanted Michael and Linda to be lifelong partners. It just didn't happen that way.

Instead, I was completely lost. I knew I could go get a job, I knew more companies than ever needed my corporate expertise, so I had confidence and faith in my ability. What really stung was that for years I'd been a really successful leader and now I was looking behind me and there was hardly anyone following. That was a big piece of my bargaining chip with potential partners, and now it was gone. Not only did I have to start over again, but I didn't have but a few people with me. The stress and anxiety began to kick in. "Holy shit," I thought. "What am I going to do now?" The definition of insane is doing the same thing over and over and expecting a different result. That's exactly what I was doing.

I sat in the stairwell of our rented home in Texas completely lost. I remember my poor wife having to be my counselor and suggesting maybe I try something else. I was sitting there pointing at the industry going, "It works! Look at this company. Look at that company. It can work. It's possible." But was it ever really going to happen *for me?* When LifeCore/LifeFX Global fell apart I had no idea where to go or what to do. How many times can you be defeated? How many times can you get knocked down and still get up and go forward? I had no answer.

It was one of the heaviest, darkest moments of my life.

CHAPTER 10

isXperia

can't quite say why I kept pushing forward in the direct sales industry every time it seemed like I had hit rock bottom. No matter the stop, I could always point to one thing here or another there as to why it hadn't worked out for me. Looking back, all those things were my steppingstones, but at the time they were just reasons why I should keep trying. I had seen direct sales work and I was determined to prove it could work for me. When I was moving on from Acquire Benefits Group or Burn Lounge or bHIP, there had been this pent-up pressure to get on a limb and find the next thing. I always had this huge following behind me, and I knew I had to make a decision quickly because every day that I didn't there was potential to lose one of my people. As I sat in my stairwell pleading with my wife after LifeCore Global, I didn't have any of that. I wanted to start up again, but I felt like I didn't have as much to bring to the table as I had previously.

Vince Filippone Jr. was one of a small number of people who I felt was still with me when LifeCore Global went down, but I could feel him and the few other people that were still standing by my side starting to second guess me. Vince had followed me from Acquired Benefits Group to LifeCore Global and we had a lot of fun working together. He was sharp and witty, had a great personality and we had a lot in common.

I thought the world of Vince, and in the several times I stayed at his house, I could tell he and his wife, Whitney, had mutual feelings about me as well. He was a great running companion who you could count on. But while Vince was still there with me in the weeks after LifeCore Global, I could feel, without him saying anything, that he wasn't quite listening to me as he had before. Nonetheless, he looked like he was still present and tried to introduce me to a company named ViSalus that was growing at breakneck speed.

I wanted nothing to do with ViSalus. This was a great example of one of those MLM junkie companies that I had seen from afar, and during my bHIP steppingstone I learned a valuable lesson that while they might work for some people, it wasn't for me. I didn't know ViSalus, but their CEO was the stereotype of someone who enters the industry who isn't familiar with it and doesn't understand the culture. Blythe Inc. purchased ViSalus, infused a bunch of capital and kept ViSalus going. Aside from the CEO, the other two co-founders came with experience and knowledge of how direct selling organizations are built.

I saw what ViSalus did and how they built their culture, and it was the part of direct sales that I didn't like and to this day still can't stand. I remember watching a video of one of the co-founders teaching promoters at ViSalus how to seek and destroy smaller and weaker direct selling companies, by targeting and stealing their promoters to bring them over to ViSalus. It created the mentality and type of culture that is why so many of these companies come and go so fast. That's how MonaVie had become so big. MonaVie had raided Amway with the same type of culture, people who are accustomed to jumping from one company to the next. I'm not trying to demean anyone, but it is what it is. They're going to find something fancier down the road and leave you hanging. While MonaVie's product was crap in my opinion, they were as good as it gets in terms of marketing. The way they presented their product and the way they branded MonaVie was one of the best-looking global direct sales companies at that time. They were so successful they got close to generating $1 billion a year in sales. But just as MonaVie had been built up by raiding a competitor, they came crashing down when ViSalus employed the same tactic against them. ViSalus had begun dismantling MonaVie at a very fast rate and was gaining traction. Now ViSalus was the hot ticket and had quickly become one of the shiniest lures in the direct selling industry.

I knew there was nothing for me at ViSalus. I had figured out these types of companies and seen how this method works, creating the crazy initial climb of revenue. But it isn't sustainable if you're not building an organic business with authenticity, culture, and people passionate about a product line. It's got to be all about the product.

You're going to go out of business when some other company comes and raids your sales force, and that's exactly what happened with MonaVie and then eventually ViSalus. The sales force that had migrated from Amway to MonaVie was now at ViSalus, and when you jump ship that many times in this industry, every time you move you lose credibility and followers. Do it two or three times in a row and you don't have hardly any horses left in your barn. It was just a raiding of the database to bring people over, which caused this crazy rush, but when that dust settled they were gone because it wasn't a product-driven business.

That's the ultimate difference in companies like ViSalus or MonaVie versus ones like Avon or Mary Kay. Those long-term ones aren't about getting rich quick, they're not about the Ferrari. They're not about the flash. It's a ton of passionate people who really, really like your product. I'm not saying MonaVie or ViSalus were run by bad people—their intentions were probably great (outside of teaching promoters how to raid other companies)—but it was one of the saddest things I've seen in this industry to watch ViSalus claim to reach $700 million a year in sales and basically be out of business years later. Vince was trying to get me to go to ViSalus, and once he connected with them, they were trying to get me on calls. I never took any of them or had any interest. I had made a lot of progress as an executive, had been the president of two companies, and I wasn't going to take a step backward and start at the bottom all over again, which is what it would have been with Vince and ViSalus. I had a gut feeling Vince and the others were going on without me, and they had to do what was best for them, which I appreciated. But I needed to do what was best for me as well.

Before Vince left my barn with all the others, he had introduced me to Christopher Bratta, who was the CEO of a nutritional product company called isXperia. The first time I met Christopher, he wined and dined me in Fort Myers, Fla., where he explained that he had gotten isXperia up and running and gladly admitted he wasn't the best or most well-versed CEO. "I'm well aware of who you are and your capabilities," he told me. "I need a president. I need somebody that can build the marketing, that can build the company." When Christopher and I met, I had no following with me and I was burnt out on building teams and driving sales. By now, I had been through everything you could imagine in direct sales. I'd met all these people and seen all these red flags. I could see that isXperia wasn't awful but was in disarray, and Christopher clearly wasn't a great leader. My options were limited, but I also had some leeway to make demands. I told Christopher I was happy to join his corporate team and could do all those things he said isXperia was lacking, but I wasn't going to drive sales. I had gone through so much shit in the previous few years and couldn't stand the thought of getting on a conference call and being the rah-rah guy.

One of the biggest lessons at isXperia and throughout all of my stops at other companies—every single one of them—is that if you're going to be successful in direct sales you have to build your own software. Probably 95 percent of direct selling companies do not have their own software platform. There are basically three main software providers in the industry and each of them service thousands of companies a month. This creates a bottleneck, and turnaround times on the simplest things, like wanting to launch a "Free Shipping" promo one weekend, takes so much time. It's inefficient and burdens companies so much. I decided if I ever had my own company, I was going to build my own software. The biggest positive about my time at isXperia was also one of my biggest discoveries. I still remember doing a Saturday training event for isXperia and meeting a young kid named Justin Rouleau. Justin and his wife,

Sarah, were distributors of isXperia, and Justin was probably 20 years old at the time. He was young with his eyes full and so motivated. I remember the leaders in the field showing me all the marketing assets Justin was building by himself. Websites and cool marketing stuff online. It was far superior to what our own IT team at isXperia was doing. I ended up hiring Justin to our IT team and we clicked from Day 1. It turned into a very effective relationship where I would brainstorm initiatives and Justin could pull it off. It was one of the few positives of isXperia.

What I learned early on during my time at isXperia was that Christopher was one of those people who told you anything you needed to hear at the moment. He never worried about the consequences of overpromising. He was so focused on trying to get the company going that he was going to say "Yes" to everything, hoping he'd figure out a way to clean things up and iron out all the wrinkles when he had to deliver. That's what ultimately ruined the company. As dismal as the turnaround results were, we did in fact grow the company. It wasn't a homerun by any means, but when I got there, the company's sales were around $100,000 a month. When I exited approximately 10 months later, they were around $500,000 a month. We had things going in the right direction, but unlike with LifeCore Global and all these other companies where I was willing to ride things out and go down with the sinking ship, I knew very early on that Christopher's way of telling people what they wanted to hear was destructive. There was no way I could truly turn around the company as one step forward resulted in two steps back. Christopher was continuing to destroy the growth with how he operated. Part of my compensation at isXperia came through bonuses and overrides on sales, and Christopher had stopped paying them to me for around six months. He owed me nearly $100,000 by the time I finally confronted him. I was tired of being a "team player" and believing his words, which were always, "I'll get it to you next month." When that never materialized, I hit him hard, and he essentially pushed me out. It all made sense, "Oh, wow, he's been strategically planning this." I was caught off-guard. The whole thing eventually turned into a big lawsuit and just like that I was done with another direct sales company.

I started to ask myself: Am I myself turning into a direct selling junkie?

When Christopher and I split, I was in complete disarray and had more anxiety in my life than ever. I was deflated. I was confused. I've always been a determined and motivated person, but my spirit was beaten. I was getting older in life and was no longer quite as vigorous. It was no longer as easy to be that dreamer I'd always been and I came very, very close to quitting on direct selling once and for all. That was my make-or-break moment where either I went against the status quo and truly accomplished what I had always wanted to or I just turned around and settled for the normal life that I had long rebelled against. When isXperia was done and I was sitting there looking at myself in the mirror and talking with my wife, it was so obvious: There were no other choices to be made, nobody else to partner with, no other companies to look for. I knew too much now, there were no excuses. I had to go do it myself. "Jason, you know what's next. You need to start your own damn company and jump out of the fucking plane. Jump, pull the parachute and let's go do this."

As nervous, anxiety-riddled and completely lost as I was, it was very apparent what was next in my life and that was to go start my own company. I knew way too much. I say this respectfully to every person I've been in business with, but I knew I was better than every one of them. Even Christopher, when he was trying to talk his way out of owing me almost $100,000, was trying to say, "Jason, you're the most talented person I've ever had. Why are you even working for somebody like me? Go start your own company." It was like, "You have all the answers, Jason." I knew how to manufacture the product, I knew about the compliance, the regulatory, the marketing. Now I knew I could create the software. It was almost like I had been pushed to this situation. I'm certainly not perfect, but I'm a man of faith, and I know what has happened in my life is much bigger than just me as a person. For whatever reason, I feel like I have been protected and guided to get where I am today. I'm not stupid enough to say what has happened in my life is just because I'm so great.

And in this moment, I had a feeling of, "You gotta do it, Jason. You're here for a reason. The time has come."

I didn't have a ton of capital behind me, and I was by myself, but I knew it was go-time. Anybody that's started their own business for the first time knows it's nerve-racking. What was really hard was that my resume wasn't loaded with massive wins and now I was taking the ultimate leap to the next stone. There would be no one I could point the finger at. There wouldn't be a Christopher to blame as the reason the company failed; there wouldn't be compliance issues like at Burn Lounge to point at for the company's demise; or bHIP to look at and say they didn't care about marketing or innovation.

You may wonder as a reader—as I did while living it—whether I was just someone passing blame each time things didn't go well? As I've taken time to reflect, what I realize is that each time I've been through these challenges I've been handcuffed by something out of my control. But from each of those moments came a lesson I would one day use.

Now it was time for all those lessons to come into play. If I failed now, the only person to blame would be me.

CHAPTER 11

Going Solo with POWDRemix

As certain as I was about what was next, I felt paralyzed as I sat on the back of the proverbial plane, cruising at an altitude of 18,000 feet and running out of time to make my jump. Sometimes in life you know exactly what you need to do and yet you still have to summon the courage to take the leap of faith or risk missing out. I needed to jump off this plane, go on my own and see where I landed. But I was just deflated from all the defeats. It probably took me 45 days to build up the confidence to do something else, to start my own thing. Thank the Lord I kept going.

What was so nerve-racking was going alone. There was no bad partner to blame. I would be making every decision there was to make. Setting up the merchant account? That was on me now. Paying commissions on time? Me. My product better be successful. I would be in control of each decision and accountable for every outcome. And would others join me? It was very tough. When I finally decided, "OK, I'm going to go for this," I didn't have bottomless pockets backing me up. I had to make it work by myself, bootstrapping it. I didn't think I would need a lot of capital to get started.

How the manufacturing world works is you place purchase orders and, depending on the relationship you have with the vendor, you get certain terms, if any. Depending on what your terms are, the invoice for your product isn't coming for 30-60 days. I had become well versed at being able to launch these companies quickly and generate sales fast. Starting a business is always a risk, but I felt like I knew the formula and had some built-in time to make it work. I knew the industry well, and the ideas were already spinning in my head. I had great relationships with manufacturers and, above all else, I had a secret weapon in my back pocket.

One of the biggest things was the software-cloud technology. When I left isXperia, Justin had called me. We had built a good relationship working together. He was your stereotypical IT guy—a man of few words, stuck to himself and banged away at the computer—but when he called, he was direct. "I'd like to go wherever you're going," he told me. I didn't have a lot of answers for him at the time but told him I'd call him when I did.

One thing I had learned at isXperia and through my time at all of these other companies is that if you're going to be successful you have to build your own software. I knew I needed software and Justin was just the person to help put it together. I called Justin when I finally picked myself up off the ground and began moving forward. I told him my plan to start a company and that I wanted him to run the IT team.

Before the isXperia rollercoaster, I had earned six-figures for multiple years prior. Although things like Acquire Benefits Group was a failure and LifeCore Global didn't work out, I always made money. It wasn't set-you-up-for-life money, but I wasn't destitute like my days in Nashville eating canned tuna. I had saved up money, but my reserves had grown thin because Christopher owed me $100,000 from not paying me for several months coupled with paying legal bills to chase that debt. Tracy worked for a company, MultiView, where she made $60,000-$70,000 a year.

As I looked to start this next venture, I absolutely knew I had to build out the software platform, which would be the cloud technology and foundation of a great company. But when it came time to pay Justin for his early programming work, I had to do something that was extremely difficult for me: Ask Tracy to write a personal check for $2,400 to pay him. I had proposed selling my Corvette to pay Justin, but Tracy was adamantly against it. "No, you're not selling it," she told me. "We're going to pay our one employee." I still vividly remember watching her write the check. I had never in our relationship asked her for financial help. I knew being an entrepreneur wouldn't be easy. Still, I learned quickly why it's not for everyone. I can't explain the amount of stress and sleepless nights I felt in those months. If you're someone who wants low stress and low pressure in life, and always to be guaranteed a paycheck by Friday, you're best off getting a job and working for somebody. I'm not complaining. I chose this path. But the road to success in business isn't always glamorous. Anybody who doesn't believe me just has to look at the 15 years it took just to get to this moment, where I still hadn't fully realized my dreams.

As I was beginning to research products, what I was going to do and how I was going to do it, Justin was vigorously building out the software. My strongest manufacturing connection in the industry was with a gentleman named Jerry Sterris, and I wanted to focus on the concept of premium, powder-based beverages. Anything that could be put in a stick pack or a packet—a protein shake, an energy drink, a powder for joint support, a powder for sleep, etc. Anything that could be dumped into water, shaken and consumed was my business model. Our two-person operation became POWDRemix. The first three products we manufactured were a healthy energy beverage, a sleep powder and a meal replacement shake. Within the first 30 to 60 days in business, I was emailing my Rolodex about POWDRemix. I was at the lowest point in terms of my following—and my spirit, truthfully, was beat—but I was still sludging forward. While I was willing to keep going forward, a lot of people had certainly thrown in the towel on direct sales and probably on Jason Camper, too. I've always been proud that whether I was broke, wealthy or somewhere in between, I've maintained who I am as a person. I've treated people right and been a person of character. Although many people had thrown in the towel on following me to this new startup company, I was still thought of and regarded as a stand-up person.

Included in my mass emailing was Paul Gravette. I didn't know Paul very well at the time, but we had crossed paths when I flew with Brian after Burn Lounge to Dallas to take a look at joining forces with Drink A.C.T. That was before we ended up starting bHIP with Terry. Our time with Paul had been short-lived, but we kept in touch over the years, exchanging text messages and emails cheering each other on in our endeavors. I didn't know it at the time, but when Paul received my email, his wheels started immediately turning. Not long after he received my email blast, Paul started calling me and inquiring about POWDRemix. Casual phone calls quickly turned into very aggressive conversations. Today, Paul and I have a brotherly relationship and Tracy refers to him as my second marriage. But when I first met him, Paul was "very energetic." He would call me, no joke, 15 or more times in a day. Sometimes, I'd get off the phone with him minutes earlier and my phone would ring again with him calling right back. "Hey, what are your thoughts on this?" he'd ask, before realizing I was tied up with work. "OK, do your thing. Do your thing. I'll catch you later." I've never experienced someone that wanted to interact so much. It wasn't a bad thing, but it had me wondering if there was an angle I wasn't seeing.

As it turned out, he was really intrigued with my cloud-based software and all the moving pieces. Everything about POWDRemix looked so good to him, but he wasn't being very direct with me. He was beating around the bush, but he had seen what I had done and accomplished with POWDRemix in a short period of time. He saw I was building state-of-the-art infrastructure and saw potential for a collaboration. He wouldn't say what he was really interested in. Lots of questions, but no direction of what he was really thinking.

I remember getting off the plane in Nashville one day and I had multiple voicemails from Paul. We had been talking shop for close to a month about what we felt would make the world's best direct sales company, what had worked in his past, what worked in my past and what challenges we had seen along the way in our journeys. We had similar stories. I walked out of the terminal at Nashville International and called him. "Are you and I going to start a business or what?" I asked him bluntly. "You're calling me 30 times a day but you're never really telling me what you want or what you're thinking." He was caught off guard. It was the elephant in the room.

That's how *the* Le-Vel conversation finally began. We started discussing his background and my background, what he was looking for and what I was looking for. I felt I had found the formula to success in the industry, but Paul wanted to start fresh. "I don't want to do POWDRemix because that's you and everybody already knows that," he told me. "I would be coming in as a little brother. I would like to sit down and see if there's a possibility of starting something together from scratch."

It was one of the hardest decisions I've ever had to make in my life. I had just started a company, my company, and I was already starting to get my name out there. At the same time, I had this feeling of being so beat up. Not only had I felt so defeated, there was no one helping me. POWDRemix had been me and Justin. He was doing IT and I was doing everything else. So in those early discussions with Paul talking about what a perfect company looked like, what was important to both of us and if there was a way for us to collaborate, really the only thing that attracted me at that moment was the thought of having some help. I was dying for a breath of air, and the thought of having someone to work with was the only thing that made me consider starting all over yet again.

POWDRemix hadn't even been in existence for six months when Paul asked me to go off and start something new. I could see potential in me and Paul creating something and truly having the perfect partner was my dream. But I could also see a ton of risk. I didn't really know Paul that well. POWDRemix was by no means successful yet, but it was starting to grow. There were people ordering, things were happening. So I had a decision to make. You might not be reading this book if I hadn't made the decision I did. It turned out, POWDRemix wasn't really about starting a business in this industry. It was perfecting the operations that would eventually lead to a multi-billion-dollar business down the road. Not only did POWDRemix have the cloud-based software, it was developing operations, customer support, paying commissions, logistical integration, engineering of nutritional formulas—we were truly testing everything. It was almost like POWDRemix essentially served as a soft opening for Le-Vel. I didn't see it that way at the time, but that's exactly how it went down in the years that followed.

Think about this: If you wanted to launch a restaurant in New York City, right in Times Square, and it's going to be the busiest, the biggest, most successful restaurant in New York, you would decide to open it a month in advance to iron out all the kinks, figuring things out and getting the kitchen dialed in. By the time you have your official launch, that restaurant is humming. That's really what happened with POWDRemix. During those six months, we identified problems with our integrations with the shipping company, we identified problems with the payment processing company, we built the commission calculations, we did everything. I still have a Facebook message from Paul that he sent in 2011. "Hey, let's catch up soon." A few weeks after I had called him, Paul and his son drove to Dallas. When we finally got together, not only did I know more than I could ever have known on how to build and operate these companies, I had the engine. I had the V12 Lamborghini cloud-based infrastructure ready to go.

The biggest thing about POWDRemix was it pushed me off the plane. I was sitting on the edge with my parachute, I'd never jumped out of a plane and I was scared to do it, my knees were shaking. Everybody was telling me it's going to be OK. My gut was telling me it was time to start my own company. But it was the scariest decision. It was one of the most impactful things that has happened in my life. Had I not jumped off that plane, the cloud-based technology would have never been created, the operations that run a company approaching $3 billion in sales would have never been established. You likely would not be reading this book.

Maybe POWDRemix wasn't short-lived after all. It created a foundation for where I am today and taught me a valuable life lesson: Sometimes you have to take the risk, a risk many will not take, jump and see where you land.

CHAPTER 12

The Start of Le-Vel

I t was a hot April day as Paul and I sat on the pool deck at the NYLO Hotel in Irving, Texas. Paul's oldest son, Rhodes, swam nearby as we worked on our laptops around all the pens and paper scattered across the table. Paul and I had spent hours on the phone talking shop after I bluntly asked him whether we were going into business. Now it was happening. Paul had come from Nashville so we could sit down and truly start bullet-pointing, diagramming and drawing up what this partnership and business would look like. For three days we sat beside that pool scribbling down notes in the Texas heat. We kept going back and forth working through one critical question: What is the absolute perfect company?

Of course, we knew we needed a unique product. I had become well-versed and very good at being able to be the architect of a product line and, in my six months of building POWDRemix, I had added to my great relationships with manufacturers. Through all my stops in the previous 15 years, I could now sit down and say, "OK, we're going to build XYZ product. I want it to have this vitamin mineral breakdown, these amino acids and these antioxidants." It was a matter of Paul and I identifying what we felt would be the best product ever created. What would be the world's premium product line? What would it look like? What would it feel like? How would we build the Ferrari of nutraceuticals?

What a lot of people that have never been in the direct sales space or have never run a company don't get is that building a successful business is not about *one thing*. People think, "Oh, my God, if we could just find the most unbelievable product then we're going to go to the moon!" Not true. There are so many pieces to the puzzle in business. Paul and I were determined to raise the bar. Our industry has been around for a long time and businesses have tried a variety of plans to sell products. Through all my steppingstones, I knew with 100 percent certainty that you could have the greatest product on Earth but, if there was a crack in the foundation, it didn't matter. Burn Lounge and Acquire Benefits Group both had products that set the world on fire. But one didn't have its ducks in order and the other made a critical infrastructure mistake. Even at LifeCore Global, where all the boxes were checked, over-selling science had crushed what seemed like a sure-thing product.

What was special about Paul and I was we weren't two executives that came over to direct sales from another industry. It wasn't like we were really successful in the automotive realm and then said, "Oh, just because we're successful over here, we know we're going to be successful over there." We both came from the trenches. We knew what it was like to be in the field as a distributor. So when Paul and I had those early conversations of what the perfect company would look like, we were able to answer the question so eloquently. It was all about identifying what we felt were high-impact products that people could share, take and consume easily, our feelings on what drives behavior on the promoter side and what's important to culture. It was more about high-level discussions and, as it turned out, we were very much on the same page. We were so aligned in our beliefs and what we wanted to do and what we knew could be done. It quickly became clear we had enormous potential.

We didn't solve everything sitting poolside, but that's where we really started putting the pieces together. We knew we had this incredible software that was integrated with all these suppliers and vendors. Why not make a story out of our cloud-based technology model that the industry had never heard of? We talked about our customer movement ideas and how we wanted to be a customer acquisition company. That's where we brainstormed the "Refer two, get your product free" model and where we discussed how we were in alignment on not making someone pay and force them into the salesforce just to purchase the product. We decided it was essential that we never charge anyone a fee to sell our products or join our company.

It drove me and Paul crazy that 99 percent of direct selling companies charged people to be a part of them. Before you could even buy the product, you had to pay their membership fee and their website fees. It was like, "Wait a minute, you're going to charge somebody to sell your product? Don't you want them to be a part of it?" Look at the biggest communities in the world—Facebook, Instagram, YouTube, Google. You don't see Google charging for a Gmail account. You don't see Instagram charging someone to post photos. We wanted to build a huge community that people wanted to be a part of. And it was going to be free. These were all things that went against the unwritten rules of the industry. We truly pieced together the best parts of our years of experiences and threw away the rest. Everything centered on those emotional buttons that made a company successful or not.

I didn't really have any concerns about the company. But despite how smoothly our discussions were going, I was still on edge about it. I had finally found something that seemed to work with POWDRemix, and my track record of working with other people wasn't exactly glowing. I didn't know if it was me or just the situations, but I had not had a lot of success partnering with people. I tried several times to run Paul off, to crush the whole idea. "This is not going to work," I remember telling him. Although I saw the positivity and potential, and it looked like we had some synergy, it was very clear we were two very opinionated people, and it appeared on the surface like we had similar skill sets.

I really worried about having two chefs in the kitchen. I was looking for every reason not to move forward, and I remember the last time Paul came to Dallas to go over the blueprints before the final decision. If you live in Dallas or anywhere around it, you know the Holy Grail is this Mexican restaurant, Mi Cocina. Ask anybody from Dallas, they've been to Mi Cocina a zillion times. The hot item is an iconic drink called the Mambo Taxi, which is their spin on a frozen margarita. One Mambo Taxi is the equivalent of three normal margaritas, but they go down with ease, they're so good. It's like a drug. The combination of their food, their salsa, and this drink, it doesn't get any better. Paul had lived in Dallas before moving to Nashville, and so when he arrived that day for our dinner meeting, he started at Mi Cocina earlier in the day to catch up with some old friends. Around 4 o'clock, Paul showed up late to my house and explained he had been catching up with friends at Mi Cocina. "Dude what's going on?" I asked him. "Why are you so late? I thought this was an important meeting." "Oh, my gosh, I'm sorry," I remember him telling me. "I just got carried away catching up with friends and lost track of time." We were in the final stages of starting our new company, but maybe I had a red flag to fall back on. I was so paranoid about making this move that everything made me second-guess. Even Tracy was worried that my new business partner had shown up to the house drastically late. Ultimately, the conversation turned where it should have. At the time, it caused concern. Looking back now, we all laugh about it.

At some point, you have to decide you're going for it no matter what. I relate teaming up to start a business to marriage. You find out who the person is, you try to check all these boxes, but you don't have a crystal ball that's going to tell you, "This marriage will be absolutely perfect with no issues at all." You may know you're in love with somebody, but you don't know that you're not going to have issues along the way. That's where I found myself in the early stages with Paul. I had some concerns. He probably had some, too. But we could feel synergy brewing and bubbling. It was almost an unspoken thought, "Are we going to do this or not?" I had two doors presented to me and I gambled on the new door. I gambled on the discussions. I gambled on Paul. I went with my gut. A lot of people probably wouldn't have made that decision; they probably would have said, "You know what, Paul, you're a great guy but, man, if only you and I could have met six months ago. I just started my company, my name is on this logo, all my chips are in on this deal and I don't see how I can throw it in park and jump out and go get in another car." But that's essentially what happened. Once I mentally shifted gears, I was done with POWDRemix and on to the next thing. Paul and I were now partners, here comes Le-Vel.

What became very obvious early on is that while Paul and I have the same beliefs and the same views, our skill sets are on two completely different playing fields. What Paul never told me early on was, "Jason, you and I are not in the same kitchen." We were in two totally different lanes. Paul's passion and excitement and skill set is on the front side of the company. He's one of the best that I've ever seen in the industry at working with promoters and cultivating relationships with the promoters, where my expertise is at the operations side. I'm on the back end managing the company, the supply chain, manufacturing the products, the formulations, the comp plan. He kicks ass over there and I kick ass over here. What I've learned is the yin and yang and filling in the gaps is what makes the perfect business partnership. We're never bumping into each other.

Sometimes you have to take the gamble. Did I know it was going to become a multi-billion dollar company? Of course not. We don't have a crystal ball to help us make decisions in life. But any reservations I had couldn't top what was looking really good in terms of our strategy and alignment.

OUR NEW COMPANY STARTED as an underdog story. We had a grand total of $130,000 and three employees: Me, Paul and Justin. I don't even know if there's a way to run a leaner operation than we did in those early days. It was wild how Paul and I all of a sudden launched this business but, ironically, it was very easy despite some of our limitations. While POWDRemix had only been in business for six months, it had ironed out all of the kinks a new startup might otherwise have. We identified problems with integration with the shipping company, we sorted out issues with the payment processing company and we built the commission calculations. POWDRemix was essentially a trial ground for the entire operation platform and became the software platform that flawlessly ran the entirety of our new company from Day 1. And still does to this day.

What also helped jump-start our new company was that I could roll over the product line from POWDRemix. I had all these incredible formulas in the bag and, with being in the direct sales space for 15 years by then and dealing with manufacturing companies, I had built a lot of great relationships and become well-versed in the manufacturing space. All three products that we initially launched are still sold in high volume today. When it came to our product line, there were two non-negotiables. First, we knew we didn't just want a great product, we wanted to create an experience. Second, our product had to be made with superior ingredients and be absolutely premium. Sadly, that is not the standard for 98 percent of the health and wellness products in the industry, in my opinion.

When we started the company in 2012, I told Paul, "If we're going to do this, if I'm going to put my name on this product, and we're going to give it everything we have, I want to be the Ferrari of nutrition." Our cost of goods would be higher and we weren't going to have as much profit built in. But when somebody took our product, they were going to feel it, they were going to notice it and therefore they were going to have more brand loyalty. Nobody ever feels their vitamins, right? We were going to have a different experience. Our efficacy was going to be night and day different than all the other health products trying to make a quick buck. We knew if we built a better product our retention was going to be five times better than the other companies where somebody would take their product and never buy it again because they didn't experience anything.

We came up with the name for that product line and experience before we settled on a name for our new company. Paul had a potential product line name on the tip of his tongue: "Thrive." I thought it was absolutely brilliant. I'm a marketing guy, and it made complete sense. I remember looking on Google for the word Thrive and there was hardly anything out there. You'd find maybe a couple general results on the Internet about Thrive and not necessarily in the nutrition space. Today if you searched on Google for Thrive supplements, Thrive is us. But before we adopted Thrive, it was a name nobody had really capitalized on. It was the perfect name. We started coming up with the Thrive Experience, the three steps people take within 40 minutes of getting out of bed in the morning on an empty stomach. It's simple and it's easy, and that system remains today as our No. 1 selling product. We felt we had captured something with that nutritional system, combined with our philosophy of premium grade ingredients and committing to efficacy and quality over quantity. Not in our wildest dreams could we have imagined it would lead to almost $3 billion in sales nine years later.

As we brainstormed names for the new company, we kept hovering around the tagline "Premium Level, Premium Lifestyle." We loved the concept of premium level. But as cool as we thought Level was, it didn't really mean a whole lot on its own. As we tossed around names, I remember talking to one of my best friends from El Paso. I brought up the tagline and explained that we didn't want to name the company Level. "Nivel," he threw out, which is Spanish for "level." It is also pronounced Ni-vel. That night I started playing with the word Level and amidst my messing around I inserted a hyphen for Le-Vel. When you're trying to come up with a company name, not only is the meaning important, but of course the .com is too. I typed in le-vel.com and it didn't direct anywhere. I searched GoDaddy and the .com was available. The next day I approached Paul. "I've got it. It sounds cool. It's a new name, it's novel, it's unique," I said. "Le-Vel.com." That was it, Le-Vel was born.

In the early days we were in a limbo period as we put all of the pieces of Le-Vel together. What I had learned from experience was the more you tell people in the early stages, the more it comes back to haunt you. Before launch, nobody can buy your product, all they can do is judge you based on what you tell them. The more you give them, the more they have time to poke holes. Meanwhile, your competition sees a new company getting ready to start up, and pre-announcing products only gives them more time to react. I was also coming out of POWDRemix, and if you did a search for "Jason Camper," it might give you pause. "Wait a minute, isn't he associated with this other company? Wasn't he with LifeCore Global?"

I remember one of the early conference calls, and both of us were nervous about people doing a search and becoming confused about POWDRemix. Paul started the call and as he began to introduce me, he said, "This is my business partner... Simon." At that time, I was officially quiet and behind the scenes. As top leaders started to emerge and build the biggest teams, we started secretly giving them samples. We still didn't want a lot of interaction with the masses just yet, and people didn't know I was involved. One of our early leaders was a woman named Toni Strathman, who would later become one of our millionaire award recipients. Toni lived in Dallas, so I put samples of the product in a plastic bag, hung it in a tree in the back of a Kohl's parking lot, took a picture and sent it to her! All the secrecy set off a wave of commotion between a bunch of women and this rumor started bubbling that the *Secret Simon*, the other Le-Vel founder, might actually be Simon Cowell. People didn't know a whole lot about us, and as funny and goofy as the rumor was, the sales force found it intriguing because everyone thought it was so cool. Years later, Tracy and I ended up getting a dog and were trying to figure out the name. Guess what it became?

After we reached July/August 2012, we let the cat out of the bag on our first product, which was the Thrive lifestyle capsules. We didn't sell them on being part of the system, because that would have spoiled even more, but we let people know about the product, which today is the first step of the Thrive Experience. While the company was still in the early pre-launch phase, we ran a promo: Enroll 10 new free accounts this week and we'll send you a sample. That's when things started getting really interesting. People were experiencing our new product and having really good results. There was a buzz around Le-Vel and Thrive. In that pre-launch period we were enrolling 6,000 new accounts each day. I had seen an incredible pre-launch at Acquire Benefits Group, but Le-Vel topped it.

Everything was just about ready. Manufacturing and production was in place, the technology stack was built out and word was getting out. Up until now there had only been a few hints about what was coming. We pre-launched the company under a domain called The LV Life. We had not told anybody the company name, the Thrive product name or idea behind the nutritional system (Thrive Experience). We were this secretive company gearing up to launch. In September 2012, we flipped the switch.

We definitely weren't a rocket ship out of the gates. We only generated around $350,000 in sales during our first full month in business. Contrast that with the first month at Acquire Benefits Group, where we brought in $1.8 million in the first 24 hours

With all the buildup in sign-ups during the LV Life pre-launch, we had been expecting to generate seven figures right out of the gate. It wasn't diffusing. We still had a lot of positive signs and a lot of interest, we just didn't have the big conversion we were expecting. We had put thousands and thousands of people in the system during our pre-launch and had worked the numbers and scenarios. If even 20 percent of the people converted from a free account to a paid account the day we went live, our projections had shown a much higher number. It was a bit of a letdown, but we were still very optimistic. We kept going and pushing out our products. By the end of the first year, we had generated just under $10 million in sales. That's when some concerns began to emerge. Was this going to take off or not? We had both been here time and time again before and knew you couldn't sit there on the launch pad for too long and not take off. In business, there's a real fragile moment where you can only go so long telling everybody, "It's gonna go, it's gonna go, we're in the early stages."

That's when Paul started getting antsy. He has three kids and was supporting his family, and we weren't making a lot of money. When we started Le-Vel, Paul and I agreed to a budget that paid us $1,000 per week, but many weeks we wouldn't get paid. We were so frugal, because we were used to companies where you weren't sure if you're going to get a commission the next day or not. We held on to every penny and made every penny go as far, wide and long for the company as we could. We had seen the here-today, gone-tomorrow scenarios. I had been through Acquire Benefits Group and Burn Lounge and had seen a quick rise and then a burn down. I remember Paul calling me up. "Hey, I've got this and that going on with the kids and Leigh Ann, she's kind of on my case right now. If it's possible, can you wire me some money?" I'd look at the books, and it was either, "No problem," or "No, we're treading water right now, I really can't, give me 10 days." We weren't living the Hollywood lifestyle. What was worrisome for me in that first year wasn't necessarily, "Am I going to make enough money to pay my bills this month?" As many sleepless nights as that causes, the biggest concern for me was, "If this goes wrong, what do I do next?" I had already had a bunch of failures strung together. Sure, I learned a lot, but I felt like I was running out of cards. I was running out of plays in my book. How many times can this happen? That was the scariest thing. I was addicted to sleeping pills because I was so stressed out, I couldn't go to sleep at night, my head would start running. If this doesn't work out, what was I going to do? I had to make Le-Vel work.

As the stress of the first year wore into late 2013, Paul told me he wanted to introduce me to a group from San Jose that was interested in buying Le-Vel. "No way," I told him. "I'm not throwing in the towel. This deal is too early."

"Look, just meet these people," Paul reassured me. "They're really good people."

Paul had worked with them before—in fact they had purchased a company he had previously founded. So at his request I flew to meet a guy named Rudy Revak and his business partner, Mary Julich. Rudy was in his mid-60s and had been in the direct sales industry for years. Paul thought the world of him and they did have a lot of infrastructure behind them. Their pitch was they would acquire Le-Vel, keep it under their umbrella and Le-Vel would still be Le-Vel. Thrive would still be

161

Thrive and we would continue under a new roof. I'm a numbers guy, and I remember talking to Mary back and forth about the valuation. The last email I got from her shocked me: $500,000.

Could I really give up all this for a measly $500,000? I didn't want to do it.

CHAPTER 13

To Sell or
Not to Sell?

The crossroads moment for Le-Vel came as I sat in my pickup truck in my garage after flying back from San Jose. Nothing was really glamorous right then and I could feel Paul's focus slipping away.

"If this doesn't take off, what do I do next?" I wondered to myself after the low-ball offer to sell the company. I spent the flight home trying to mentally unpack everything. I didn't know if I was about to lose my partner. I didn't know if Le-Vel was going to keep going. Incredible unknowns. Yet oddly enough, the trip was a pivotal moment for me. As I sat in my truck, I had this epiphany. I did what Paul wanted me to and heard these people out. Now I had come back ready to fight. I told myself: "No, I'm not selling this company. I'm not partnering with them. I'm digging my f—ing heels in." I knew we had something good. Yeah, it wasn't perfect yet, but let's roll up our sleeves and let's give it everything we've got.

Right there in my truck, I picked up the phone and called Paul.

Starting a business definitely isn't easy, as you can tell from my story. You don't just start companies, put them on autopilot and watch the success unfold. It takes experience, knowledge and some luck along the way. As the old saying goes, the more experience you have, the luckier you get. I'm not afraid to admit we've had luck on our side with Le-Vel. There are certainly a number of good decisions we've made over the years at Le-Vel that have set us up for success. My experience and Paul's experience go a long way, but at the end of the day you need a little luck on your side, too. I'd say 90 percent of the companies that start in this industry don't make it past one year. The reason a lot of companies don't make it primarily falls down to experience and knowledge in the industry. They're typically run by people who don't have the appropriate knowledge or experience in the space, and because of that they're not making the right decisions on what to do with the company, how to do it, what products to have, what compensation to have and so on. It's like being in the ocean with a boat, charting very rough waters, and it's critical that each decision you make is the appropriate one to keep that ship afloat. All the critical decisions you make each day, the path you choose, keeps the ship in safe waters and keeps the company growing. And if a company is owned and run by an experienced and educated management team and they still don't make it, *typically they just don't get it*. They might be great at operations, shipping products, handling customer support and successfully managing a business, but they're not good at the "wow" factor. Or they have a subpar product or subpar model. They're good people, but they're trying to launch a Honda in a Ferrari marketplace and it just never gets the attraction that it needs to succeed. Those are typically the reasons I see companies fail. When we launched in 2012, we certainly weren't the best that's ever been in direct sales, but we were really damn good. That's what made even thinking of giving up so hard after one year.

Rudy and Mary in San Jose wanted to buy majority control of Le-Vel. They had other direct selling companies in their portfolio, but I think they viewed those as being outdated and needed help from a marketing perspective to provide a spark. They had been watching what we were doing at Le-Vel, saw we had skills and assets they didn't have and wanted to retrofit their companies with new trends and marketing ideas. They saw our out-of-the-box ideas and our cloud-based technology and they wanted to buy it. Quite frankly, I think they also saw that we were going to grow even more than Paul and I were seeing at the time. But what I've learned in business is that you can really only successfully chase one rabbit. When I see models that are a boutique, family office operation with multiple direct selling companies in their portfolio, they're all just mildly successful. It doesn't fly when you try to hit multiple home runs at the same time. A successful business comes when you put all your effort, all your commitment and all your passion into one thing and are trying to go out and hit *one* home run.

Rudy and Mary wouldn't have bought just Paul's equity in Le-Vel. They wanted to buy the whole business, take control of it or buy nothing at all. But even if we didn't sell Le-Vel, I might lose Paul to their management team. Paul came to me and said: "I've got to do what's best for me, Jason. I have to pay bills and take care of my family. They're offering me a steady, six-figure salary to come oversee sales." I wasn't quite sure what direction Paul would go if we didn't sell.

But I would have absolutely kept going on my own, because I had a gut feeling. I felt like I was about to crack this new product I was working on called Derma Fusion Technology and felt like we were getting ready to put a Ferrari on the racetrack. It wasn't like I was absolutely right and Paul was wrong in the moment. He had a good history with these people, and while he probably agreed that their offer to buy Le-Vel wasn't really the right number, I think he saw upside with them and a possibility we could grow a more successful company if we had additional help and capital. I didn't see it that way. Call me stubborn, but I didn't feel like we needed the help. I knew we had something on our hands that could succeed. What was that something going to be? It was definitely going to be something more than $500,000. That's what I knew unequivocally.

ONE THING PAUL AND I have always had in common is we both like to be novel in everything we do in life. It's not very fun wearing the same shoes that everybody else in the country has or driving the exact same car, with the exact same paint as five neighbors down your block. The me-too, copycat thing has never interested me. So when we sat down to build Le-Vel it was all about being creative and novel and innovative at every chance we had. We wanted to do something that had never been seen from a product perspective. We wanted to do something that had never been done from a formula perspective. We wanted to do things differently with our comp plan. We were going against the grain from the get-go. Being different and trying to disrupt the status quo can have its challenges. There will always be people that question your ways or new ideas, but you have to be willing to tune it out and keep pressing on.

We faced a lot of criticism from so-called "industry experts" on our cloud-based technology, which was the whole idea that made Le-Vel go. In 2012, the thought of launching a business and not having a corporate office, not having a corporate address, not having a brick-and-mortar that people could drive to, go in, shake your hand—people just didn't get it. Hate is a strong word, but I truly despise corporate offices. The last thing I want to do as a human being in the morning is get up, get dressed and go to some stupid office when I could do the same work right there at my computer. I can be more productive because I don't have to talk to everybody, and I save time on the commute. Plus, in the corporate office environments I've experienced along the way, you have corporate politics, the emotion dynamics of people and wasted time with all the water cooler chitchat. When we launched Le-Vel in 2012, there had never been a 100 percent cloud-based technology operated and managed company in the direct selling space the way we were. Never.

The corporate office structure is outdated now, but we knew it in 2012. If you went to any reputable direct sales company's website you could click on the "About Us" tab where you would see a big, beautiful $20 million glass building. It was a statement: "We're credible because of this big, fancy, huge building." People scoffed at our idea of being completely in the cloud. We referred to ourselves as the first cloud-based technology company, and we had so much criticism and backlash. Critics were saying, "That air company is going to be gone overnight."

In the first several weeks of launching Le-Vel, as Paul and I pitched the product and company—who we were, who we were going to be and where we were going—the cloud-based story was one aspect where we were loud and proud. We weren't hiding from it. We didn't have the money or desire to buy a $20 million building. I wanted to put the money in the comp plan and into the product quality, not a building that I'm never going to go to. We wanted to pay more than anybody has ever paid. We wanted to launch the "Refer two customers, get your product free" program that no company in the space had ever done. We didn't want to charge website or enrollment fees. We told our promoters, "We want to put the capital into the hands of the people."

The cloud-based software that we have today at Le-Vel touches 100 percent of every operating facet in the company. There's nothing about our business that's managed or operated outside of it. With a traditional direct sales company you may have some software that tracks orders, but you typically have a finance team in-house at the office that does the payroll and a team in-house that does the commissions or does this or does that. With the software created at POWDRemix, we didn't need any of that. Everything we do with suppliers, distributors, commissions and so on is done through our technology stack. We have API integration with our warehouses, our payment processor, our commission processor and so on. Everything gets linked to the software. You've got the shipping and tracking and all the calculations from the orders that get shot through an API to the warehouse at the shipping facility. On payday, when the promoters need to get paid, all those calculations are done in the software and get pushed through an API to the pay card provider. Nothing needs to be done outside of our cloud technology ecosystem that's online. So in 2012, when we started the company, not only did we not want an office, but we also didn't need an office. In those first days, we could operate as the three-headed team of me, Paul and Justin. The software made it work. We needed personnel, but we didn't need departments or teams to execute things. What we learned is it's a more robust operating system than most traditional direct sales companies that require departments to do many of the tasks our software does. And it's cost effective.

Today, that same software technology has allowed Le-Vel to branch out with a bi-coastal shipping model. During that first year, I had a shipping partner in Salt Lake City who I worked with previously. I've always been a firm believer that you do what you do best, and you pay others to do the rest. I've seen companies get killed because not only do they try to be a direct sales company, but also, they try to be a fulfillment company and a logistics company. And now they're chasing three different rabbits and they aren't successful at any of them. I wanted nothing to do with fulfillment or logistics out of the gate because I had seen it take so many companies down. I want to run a lean and effective program. We would do what we did best at Le-Vel and pay others to do the rest. We integrated our software platform with our partner in Salt Lake City and they've handled shipping and fulfillment since Day 1, all because of our cloud technology. Since the company has grown and scaled, we've added warehouses in Memphis and Atlanta. Depending on the ZIP code of the order coming in, the software selects a designated warehouse to fill the order. Cheaper and efficient.

What the "industry experts" didn't understand at the time was the mindset of the Promoters. Our whole pitch was that we didn't need a bloated corporate office, had a capable software setup and less overheard. So we could build a better product and pay more commissions. It began resonating. The promoters weren't seeing us like the experts thought they were going to. We didn't lose any credibility because we didn't have a big, fancy building. They were all tired of the big companies. Le-Vel was an edgy, trendy, new tech company. It made complete sense to the sales force to pay them more money as a Promoter and build a better product. People flocked to us because word started circulating about Le-Vel's cloud-based technology. Less overhead, more commissions. Less overhead, higher quality of product. Other companies almost became shy about mentioning their big shiny buildings. "Oh, no, we're not spending a lot of money in a corporate environment. We're investing just as much in the comp plan and the products as those guys are." We still needed the sales to pop, but we already had something so many other companies didn't.

Buzz.

I HAD ALREADY MADE my decision about my future with Le-Vel as I called Paul from my truck while sitting in my garage. We weren't in a dispute about it, but I sensed Paul might be ready to get out from the pressure. "Man, let's just do this," he said. "Let's go for it. Let's sell the company. They can help us grow the company, we'll still make money, it will help us grow internationally."

It turned into a heart-to-heart conversation about where each of us were going and what our visions were. "No, Paul," I told him. "I'm not willing to sell my equity in the company." Neither of us had a lot of money at the time, as we had put everything into Le-Vel. Yeah, $500,000 sounded OK, but it sounded more like "now money" than it was a great business move.

I was right at the starting line with my new product named Derma Fusion Technology, which had been planned from the get-go to be the third step in the three-step Thrive Experience. We had capsules (step 1) and the shake mix (step 2) already in our product line and the DFT product would complete our third step to the Thrive Experience. We hadn't launched with the wearable nutrition product because we didn't know how to print on it and keep the ingredients active for a long enough period of time, but I was extremely close. I was working with my DFT partner and felt like any day it was going to come together. We were going to throw it into the Thrive Experience and it was going to freakin' rip. I could feel it. No other company had a wearable nutrition product like this. It was making me get up early every morning with excitement. We had only done $10 million in sales in Year 1, but our train was slowly moving forward.

We had put too much work into Le-Vel and had so many differentiators to hand it over. I leveled with Paul. After that long heart-to-heart phone call from my truck, Paul and I both decided what we had was so much more valuable than $500,000.

"Just understand, Paul, we're weeks away from announcing the Derma Fusion Technology product," I said. "So as good as now money might seem or these partners might feel, our best as a company is yet to come. I know things are financially tough right now, but we've got to hold strong. I'm telling you, this business is going to go."

As close as it might have seemed that we were falling apart, that call led to us having a stronger partnership than ever before.

That wearable nutritional technology, combined with the cloud technology, combined with the Thrive Experience, would vault Le-Vel to a multi-billion dollar company in the years that followed that phone call. We could have lost the business for $500,000. What a critical moment for us. That was the moment. The ultimate fork in the road for Le-Vel.

CHAPTER 14

DFT and the Premium Grade Philosophy

D esigning and manufacturing a product is like going to the gas station and choosing different grades of fuel for your car: regular, midgrade or premium. You can choose any of them, but you get what you pay for. That's how nutraceutical products are manufactured. You can build a fully synthetic, crap product or you can build a 93-octane premium one with the best of the best ingredients. When we plotted the path for Le-Vel, what was most important to me was launching a company with a premium-grade product philosophy. Quality equates to a really big brand and I wanted to source the best ingredients that could deliver a premium experience and results. Quality over quantity is king.

That gasoline grade analogy carries across no matter the business or industry. Companies make decisions all the time to either create premium-grade products with the best materials they can source or to cut costs and drive up their profit margins. One of the reasons we chose the route of a cloud-based company was to reduce overhead and spend more of our capital on our product. The premium-grade philosophy was essential to Le-Vel. In nutraceuticals, you have a range of choices: You can get cheap, synthetic plastic vitamins or more expensive premium pharmaceutical-grade ones. The higher grade the ingredient, the higher bioavailability, or nutritional content, that's attached to it. So when a company makes a decision to create their capsules or drink powders with a synthetic Vitamin A instead of a pharmaceutical Vitamin A, the nutritional content is night and day different. It's like comparing the performance of a Honda to a Lamborghini. A premium pharmaceutical-grade vitamin is three times more expensive on average. Again, you get what you pay for. I always tell people it's my educated guess that 98 percent of health and wellness products on any website or store shelf are synthetic. They're cheap. Most companies don't want to spend much money on quality ingredients to produce a premium product. They want to have a lower cost of goods and a higher margin. It's one of those shiny label deals. From the beginning, Paul and I were on the same page and wanted to be a Rolls-Royce in the marketplace.

Le-Vel's product line came from years of experience and from lessons I learned along my steppingstones. During my time at LifeCore Global I learned how to market a product to consumers and how not to, but I also learned what makes a product resonate. We had all the scientific data in the world to show that our product at LifeCore Global was good, but it wasn't a high impact product. If you drink a cup of coffee, 15 minutes later you're going to feel the impact. Our product at LifeCore Global was a tree bark and fish oil capsule that was supposed to offer really good longevity. The problem was, nobody could feel it. Even today, I have this incredible formula for longevity that's really, really great, but I'm hesitant to put it into the pipeline because you just don't feel it. Selling a product for weight loss, energy, mental focus or joint support is all about making things that people can feel, where they can psychologically go, "This product is working."

The premium grade philosophy made sense to people when we first started pitching the idea. I could get on a conference call with 10,000 prospective Thrivers deciding whether they wanted to start the product line or not. In 90 seconds I could go over the premium grade philosophy, tell them not all vitamins are created equal, that there is higher bioavailability with our products and, as a result, that's going to help fill in nutritional gaps and deficiencies. People get that, it makes a ton of sense. Do you want a Louis Vuitton purse, or do you want a purse from Kohl's? Do you want a steak at Applebee's, or do you want to go to Ruth's Chris? It's all about quality over quantity. The premium grade philosophy set Le-Vel apart and has been one of our biggest differentiators. Even to this day.

PEOPLE ASK ME ALL THE TIME: What aspects of the business keep you up at night? The answer today is the same as it was in 2012. The first is the safety and security of Le-Vel. We're in a heavily regulated space by the FTC and FDA and I've been through so many bad scenarios that myself and everyone on the regulatory team is constantly trying to keep the company safe. I want to be driving Le-Vel 60 mph in a 70 mph zone.

The second is innovation. I always want to be better than the competitor, so I'm always looking for that opportunity. I believe if entrepreneurs are continuously in that creative space, that's what makes them better. That's what makes a company different and unique. When you look at companies that are status quo, you can presume there's not a creative person in the room thinking, "How do we become better? What's the next product? What's the next best service?" I've pulled so many product aces out of my pocket, but they didn't happen by accident. When you're in that state of mind of always looking for the next product, you stumble upon ideas and you pursue them.

I had good formulas and products from my previous experiences. I had the premium grade belief that we were going to have better quality than the competition and we were going to spend more money for the premium grade vitamins and nutrients. But what I've learned in business is nobody has the total plan on Day 1. Sometimes things evolve and come your way. That's what has happened with Le-Vel through the years. We've done a lot of good things and developed a lot of good products, but I couldn't have told you on Day 1 that we would have all that. A lot of what Le-Vel has become was an evolution of business and things happening because we were on the lookout and focusing on being creative and innovative.

Around the time Le-Vel opened for business in 2012, I was introduced to a "frequency signal patch product" from somebody looking for a direct sales distribution channel. As an entrepreneur looking for that competitive edge and something that had never been done, I wanted to like it. At first I thought I felt an energy boost, but I was really just hopeful and euphoric. "Oh, my. If this works this could be really big." However, there was nothing legitimate or noticeable. It was more placebo-based, and it didn't work. As a marketer, I find consumers to be logical and use common sense. I didn't think I could tell someone that there's a signal on this patch, your body is picking up this frequency and it's going to make you sleep better and have more energy. I respectfully declined the product, but the wheels in my head were spinning. "If you can put a specific frequency on a patch, why not a nutritional formula?" I asked myself.

That's what put me on the warpath to pursue, "Well, if you can do that, why not put X, Y and Z ingredients on a patch?" These guys pitching me about their bogus signaling patch was what started me down the path of researching a formula and a way to create a weight loss or energy patch type of product. I didn't think if we were able to pull this off it was the Holy Grail for Le-Vel, but like any other entrepreneur in any other industry, you're always looking for the competitive edge. That's what I saw in my nutritional patch technology idea, which ended up being called Derma Fusion Technology. I saw it as the sexy lure, the competitive advantage and my mind started racing. I could see it way before I even knew how to make the product. I could tell it was going to be one of those products that people talk about. It was walking advertising. I'm a marketing guy at the end of the day. I know how to pull the right levers with consumers. When the guys with the signaling patch first approached me, I was immediately excited about their product—not because of the signaling concept, but because from the second I saw their product I saw it was a walking billboard. I didn't even know how to manufacture the patch technology yet, but I could see a woman in the salon having the DFT on and another woman going, "Hey, what's that on your arm?" "Oh, this is my Thrive wearable nutrition patch." Bam! I could envision it. I came up with the name "Derma Fusion Technology" as a cool marketing play on what would happen when you used the product. I say all the time that perception is reality, and how people perceive your company, your brand and your products creates their reality of how they think. Marketing gives you a chance to create that perception, that reality, so naming a product Derma Fusion Technology was a way to create that perception. I remember getting out of bed so excited. DFT had to work, it couldn't be all marketing. I'd sit on my computer until 3 a.m. researching and scouring the country for someone who could help manufacture this wearable nutritional technology, and the prospects were few and far between.

As a little startup company, a giant pharmaceutical company wasn't going to answer my phone call about manufacturing a nutritional patch. There's no way I could get into that door and we certainly didn't have the money they would require to take us on as a client. No one that I could find had done anything from a nutritional patch perspective. I was turning over every stone to find someone who could help me develop this product when I was talking to a friend in Florida and telling him what I was doing. He had some experience in direct selling and I remember him saying he had met a guy who was developing a patch but couldn't put it all together. He gave me the number for this guy and in the first five minutes I knew I had found the quarterback I had been seeking. I was so pumped. I've always felt your gut and intuition are the biggest indicators of if something is good or bad. I felt like this was the missing piece. If we could put this cool wearable nutrition technology together, print on it, create cool marketing sayings and logos and offer them in different colors and shapes, I knew it was going to blow up. Finally, the stress began melting away and excitement was creeping in.

It was around that time when Paul and I were offered $500,000 for Le-Vel. There was still work to do with the Derma Fusion Technology (DFT) patch, but everything looked promising. This was wearable nutrition. There was nothing else like it. The challenge we had in the early days with DFT was trying to figure out how to print on the foam substrate. When we finally solved that problem, we turned to getting the adhesive dialed in. I'm a big customer service guy, and I could see DFT not sticking on people well enough. I remember calling the team one day, "Talk to me about the adhesive. How strong is it?" Their response told me it wasn't strong enough. I didn't want anything to do with a patch that won't stick. "I want people complaining that it's hard to pull off versus it is falling off," I told them. We focused on making the adhesive super strong, and that's when everything really came together.

Developing DFT wasn't just about the patch, it was the whole system. We had the capsules, the shake and the DFT to complete the Thrive Experience. The DFT was the lure in the water. It was that attractive. Today, we have people who are trying to replicate our product. We have 27 patents and counting. It's what sets us apart. Everything we've done and everything we still do today is done with the goal of being different. I want to be the purple cow in a field of brown ones. You talk about making the right decisions in life, we could have sold the company or just thrown in the towel on Le-Vel for $500,000. DFT put us on the verge of a breakthrough.

MY TIME AT ACQUIRE BENEFITS GROUP may have been short-lived, but it wasn't a wasted opportunity. During the launch, I learned that I was really good at marketing. I had been responsible for everything surrounding that big pre-launch, building the marketing story around the concept and creating a video to share the vision. I had started writing the video script because it was part of my job, but it was through that process that it became apparent I had a marketing talent when I first worked with videographer Tony Gialluca.

When it became clear that DFT was really going to happen, I knew the launch had to be big. This was something the industry had never seen and the reveal had to match. It was in May 2013, while we were at our friends Drew and Rachelle Hoffman's wedding that I started planning the unveiling of DFT. Rachelle was a great friend of Tracy's from MultiView and I ended up hiring Drew a few years later. But working on my video script while at their wedding might not have been the most social impression! It was my first experience in Cabo, a Friday night, and everybody was drinking cocktails and enjoying themselves. There I was in the corner of the hotel room and everybody may have thought I was stuck up because I wasn't being social, which I wasn't. I was working my ass off writing the video script for DFT. The script walked people through a timeline equating what we were doing with DFT to what happened in the digital music realm when the industry went from cassette to CD to mp3 to iPod. It showcased this new level of nutritional technology. We hadn't tipped our hand about this revolutionary product that was in development. We were about to pull the DFT card out of our pocket and shock everybody. I created a website called IndustryShift.com, explaining a big shift in the health and wellness industry that was occurring from traditional nutritional products to wearable nutrition. Everything was set.

Right at that time we started preparing our people in the field for what was to come. I remember sitting in my truck with my wife waiting inside our favorite sushi restaurant, Kotta, in Frisco, Texas, doing the first conference call. We had sent an email blast telling everybody to get on the call. We said, "Something's coming. We can't fully tell you what it is because we've got some more wood to chop, but we can tell you that it's going to be as big in the nutritional space as the shift we saw from cassettes to CDs to mp3 players to iPods." That night we finally gave a sneak peek to the field, and that's when the phones started going nuts. Some people might have thought we were crying wolf, but you could hear it in our voices. It was authentic and passionate. The field just knew, "Oh, my. What are these guys up to?" It wasn't a typical conference call. It was almost like, "Get ready, start calling everybody you know right now, because when we pull the curtain back and we launch this, it's going to absolutely take off like a rocket." It was that messaging that got everybody excited. I had taken everything I'd learned about marketing and applied it for this vital launch. Going back to Apple, when they were in their hyper growth, they didn't simply launch a MacBook Pro. They would hint about how great it was going to be and how different it was and then they'd have a launch party where Steve Jobs was talking about it with the new laptop right there. They made the biggest deal out of it, which is what you should do if you have something that big. When you have a great product, you shouldn't just say, "Coming Soon: October 3." That's awful. What I did, teeing the DFT product up perfectly, building the story around it with IndustryShift.com, creating the suspense weeks before with the promoters, that created the perfect storm. We had thousands of people that came to learn about Le-Vel who had no idea who we were because of that marketing initiative.

When the video and website went live and we finally pulled the curtain back and showed everybody what our stallion product was, I felt like Le-Vel was no longer hidden. We put the DFT with our other two products, the capsules and shake, and packaged it all into an eight-week system, the Thrive Experience, that you take on an empty stomach within 40 minutes of being up in the morning, and from that moment Le-Vel started to grow. I mean it couldn't have been any better. There were thousands of people not only wanting to buy the Thrive Experience but wanting to sell it. It was simple, cool and fun. When you're an entrepreneur, that's where the passion and good feelings come from. When you see your product working in the marketplace, you see people excited, you see people adopting and accepting it, there's no better feeling. There wasn't anything cooler in the health and wellness industry. Le-Vel had come out like freakin' Batman. We were "it" from that point on.

PEOPLE SAW DFT EXACTLY like I thought they would. It was a sexy Ferrari and you couldn't test drive it somewhere else. People had experience with various supplements before, but this was so different and fun. That was the vehicle that sent Le-Vel into hyperdrive—The Thrive Experience

I learned a valuable business lesson when DFT launched. Until that point I was wearing every hat there was to wear and I was unwilling to delegate. Paul was busy on the front-end of the company doing conference calls and talking to promoters, Justin was pulling his hair out making sure the cloud technology stack held together and I was handling the supply chain, marketing, accounting, finance, customer support and all operations. While I have always been big on the customer experience, running customer support was the one role I despised. I was waking up every day trying to be positive and then my inbox was filled with negative messages like, "My box showed up damaged," even though Le-Vel had nothing to do with the damage. I still remember the support ticket that led to Le-Vel's fourth employee. The customer service tickets were driving me crazy, and I received a support ticket from this uber negative lady complaining about how her product hadn't shipped out on time. I explained that we do same-day shipping for all orders before 3 p.m. Eastern and that she had placed her order at 5 p.m., so it would go out the next day. She just wasn't practical. But in an attempt to be respectful, I said, "Sorry, we'll get this out as fast as we can." She kept beating me up. There was nothing I could say to satisfy her. I ended up crediting her shipping and she was still relentless, so I gave her a percentage off. She came back one final time nastier than she'd been the entire email chain and I told her, "It has become apparent to me that our company will never be able to meet your needs as a consumer. I have 100 percent refunded your money and I have canceled your account. Sorry, we are not the company you're looking for. Thank you so much." She responded back: "Thank you for acknowledging you're not that company. Bye-bye."

Right then I knew I couldn't do customer service. I had thrown everything I could at this lady to put a smile on her face and I was still never going to meet her needs. Not long after that, we hired Justin's cousin, Christine Fike, as our fourth employee. I was so worried that she was going to quit, and I would have to go back to customer service, that I was giving her a raise seemingly every week.

What I've learned through the growth of Le-Vel is there's always something to deal with when you're running a business. It doesn't matter what industry you're in, you're sailing a ship. Every day there's some type of storm, some choppy waves and you have to make all these critical decisions to keep sailing toward safety. That's what it was back then. It was always something, whether it was an issue we had to overcome with the supply chain and getting the inventory to the warehouse on time, working with our shipping partners to make sure they were executing effectively or trying to get commissions out on time. It was absolute chaos. At the rate sales were coming in, and for us to try to facilitate those sales and operate effectively and keep the train on the track, we couldn't have been moving any faster. We were flying 300 mph. My friends were always telling me, "Man, you're kind of not the same. You're not laughing. You're not joking." At that time, I couldn't have been any more serious because of how important the timing was of not screwing Le-Vel up. You've got one shot, you may never, ever see a scenario like this again.

During our second year in business with the Thrive Experience that now included our wearable nutrition, Le-Vel went from $10 million in sales to $100 million. We had ridden the waves through our first storm.

CHAPTER 15

Built with People & Culture

vividly remember the second getaway trip we did at Le-Vel. As with many companies in the direct selling industry, these trips have been a critical way for us to keep the energy flowing within the organization. The very first getaway we did only had 75 people in Las Vegas. But as Le-Vel hit its hyper growth, it was blowing and growing, and on our second trip we took 300 people to Cabo. Most companies have a handful of what I call ponies, or big income earners, that always get up on stage and make most of the compensation. It's the same people every time. At Le-Vel, we tried to create an inverted comp plan. Instead of continuing to reward the same people with these huge, colossal bonuses, we decided it made sense to fuel it from the bottom. Why not have more people at the bottom winning? If you build a really big team, and you have a lot of people winning on your team, you're going to be rewarded anyway. We started doing things like paying more for a car bonus and including more people in those big incentive trips, taking thousands of people to Cabo, Cancun, Las Vegas, the Dominican Republic and more. Nobody had done that in our industry.

Despite what we knew was success in those early days, we also knew how quickly a company could dry up and disappear in this business. It had happened to many others in the direct selling space. A lot of companies deteriorate and flop. I knew that as well as anybody and was on pins and needles because it had happened to Paul and I over and over. We were holding on tight, doing the best we could, trying to make the right decisions. Le-Vel was really starting to grow as I prepared to get on the stage on the patio outside of the Omni Hotel in Cabo to deliver a pump-up message during that second trip. I had the microphone in my hand and one foot on the stage, about to step up when Chad, who manages our travel, gripped my arm. I looked back and saw this frightened look on his face. "Jason," he said, "I need to talk to you really bad." This was our big moment. "Hey," I said, "I'm about to get on stage." I took another step up and Chad pulled at me again. "No," he said, "it's an emergency. I need you now." My heart stopped. I just knew. Here we go again. Everything was going well, things were working and this was it, it was all too good to be true.

As I walked with Chad toward the hotel he proceeded to tell me that hotel management had received calls because water was coming down the hallway, out of a room, and the room belonged to one of Le-Vel's promoters. Chad and hotel management had gone inside the room together where they found one of our promoters naked, underwater in a bathtub. There were medication pills spilled on the floor and alcohol everywhere. "Oh, my gosh," I thought, "someone's gonna die on our trip, and we may be responsible." It was horrible. I was about to get on stage and give my inspirational speech when the ambulance arrived and resuscitated her. She is no longer with our company, but I'll never forget that moment.

THERE IS A COMMON MISCONCEPTION surrounding direct sales that the promoters are in it to get rich. A lot of people believe everybody tries to jump into one of these companies because they think it's a get-rich-quick deal. It's the total opposite. In my years building Le-Vel, I've found that 99 percent of all promoters who enter our direct sales company actually aren't looking to get rich. Maybe there's the 1 percent of people who enter a direct sales company with hopes, goals, aspirations or even thoughts of getting rich, but most people do it to take care of a car payment, to help pay for childcare or maybe to pay off some debt. Sometimes they're really passionate about the product. It's not about these lavish goals or splashy getaways for most people. I'd estimate that 90 percent of any direct sales organization is made up of people who love the products and are interested in making an extra $200 or $300 per month to help out. Many people love being a part of the organization and being linked with the community.

Pay close attention here: I break down the industry into two categories: direct sales and multi-level marketing. Somewhere between those two is network marketing. What I consider to be a direct sales company is one that is a product-driven company culture or movement that is speaking about the product. Yes, they have a recruiting model behind that and you can enroll people, but what drives everything is a product-passionate culture. A couple of good examples of a direct selling company is Mary Kay, Avon and Rodan + Fields. I've always admired the culture Mary Kay has built. There's a reason it's still going strong after starting in 1963. Companies like Mary Kay, Rodan + Fields and Avon are all about product over opportunity. If you got on one of their calls, went to their conventions, or talked to one of their promoters, you'd hear them share about the product, how it's made them feel. The story. And, oh by the way, if you're really passionate about the product, the promoter opportunity might be for you, too.

Then you have these companies that I would put in the multi-level marketing bucket. I don't mean disrespect to any of them, they're perhaps all great people, but it's not a product-oriented movement. It's night and day in how they approach sales. Look at Amway, a company that's been in business since 1959. They're incredibly successful, and they'll be here for another 30 years or more. But historically they have been known for discussing the opportunity more than the product. Many companies that sell opportunity end up being a flash in the pan. Remember when I told you about ViSalus, a company that did over $1 billion in sales? Now they're essentially out of business a few years later. It blows my mind. If you had gone to a convention for a company like ViSalus or MonaVie one year and then returned the next, probably 95 percent of the people would be brand new because they're selling the opportunity. If someone doesn't come in and get rich, they're out, they quit. For these companies it's about the Ferrari, the RV, the vacation home. And then, oh by the way, we do happen to have a product. It's an awful environment. You have this group of top leaders that jump from company to company and circle the industry, dragging people with them. It's never about the product, they just care about the next momentum run with the new company. That's what ViSalus was, and that's why ViSalus is essentially no longer in business. The same group of people that left Amway and ran to MonaVie, then ran to ViSalus and then ran toward the next hot thing. It's never a conviction-driven culture. And who wants to be in on that?

When Paul and I set out to build Le-Vel, I knew I wanted to build a company around a product *and* a belief. That's what Thrive set out to be. I had seen these multi-level marketing companies come and go in my first decade in the industry and I had no intention of taking Le-Vel in that direction. I would define culture as passion and conviction to an idea or an ideal. When someone has conviction and passion around the product, then and only then should they consider selling it to others. Why in the world would someone go sell a product that they've never tried, have had no results with or have no conviction or passion for? They're simply promoting it as a means to make money. It's two different dynamics. If you have real culture in this space, that culture is sticky because of people's conviction, their love for the product, the mission of the company and what they believe, not because "everybody's here to get rich." I didn't want Le-Vel to be the new flavor of the month. That was ViSalus and MonaVie 101. The revolving door is a billion times larger at companies that sell opportunity than the direct selling ones like Le-Vel, Mary Kay or Avon because the bulk of people entering our company are not here to get rich. They're here because they're passionate about Thrive and the opportunity makes sense because of their conviction to the product line. If you came to one of our conventions and saw the top 100 people in our company, less than 10 percent have had experience in the industry before. They're here because of their true beliefs in the products and therefore, the business.

In the early days of deciding what we wanted Le-Vel to be, we faced a lot of questions. What mattered to us? What issues in the industry did we want to avoid? One of the big topics was how MLM-y some of these companies feel and the bad perception it creates for the industry. We wanted to be as classy as we could. So, while people don't want to get a call about an opportunity, it's very natural for anybody to want to share a product they like. When you look at Mary Kay, yeah, they're a direct selling company, but their behaviors center around women sharing the product with each other. Not, "Hey, let's go make $1 million."

I wanted Le-Vel to be seen and viewed as a customer acquisition model and I knew if we did that, we would have much greater success as a direct sales company because that's what people relate to. If 10 people set out today to go call people about an "opportunity," how many yeses would be had? Not very many, because people don't want to have those conversations. But if everybody went out and talked about the product, the opportunity will come. So many companies out there are an opportunity with a product on the back end. I hated that. I wanted Le-Vel to be a product company with an opportunity on the back end. You get many more people into the tent because they love the product. The opportunity is a natural byproduct where they're sitting there going, "Man, I love this product." They *want* to share it versus trying to convince somebody to go sell a product when they don't even know if they like it or not.

ONCE WE HAD OUR THRIVE EXPERIENCE dialed in, our focus shifted to the compensation side, and we were determined to raise the bar. Our industry has been around for a long time, and there are a lot of things that have been done, but the things we had in mind on the compensation side had truly never been done before. We wanted to pay more than anybody's ever paid. We wanted to build a program where if you refer two customers, your product is free. We wanted to let people enroll for free and not charge website fees. We were going against the grain from the get-go. It was, once again, trying to be innovative, novel and creative on all fronts and in everything we do from product to culture.

We were one of the first in the industry to not charge to be part of the company. And we were the first to offer the program where you refer two customers and your product is free. Approaching $3 billion in sales later, those innovations have made the world of difference to separate Le-Vel in the direct selling space. Ironically, that innovation was fortuitous. What you've seen since we launched in 2012 is a crackdown on federal and state regulatory guidelines. The industry has been put under a microscope and companies like Herbalife and AdvoCare have paid the price on the industry shift. Probably 99 percent of direct sales companies charge fees to buy product. When we started Le-Vel, we eliminated the fee-based system as an emotional hot button and not charging promoters in order to sell our products. We wanted to build a huge community that people wanted to be a part of and not charge them to join. The whole goal of the "refer two program" was to bring in customers, and it worked flawlessly. We've mailed out more than $200 million in free product. The reason the FTC has gone after companies like Herbalife and AdvoCare in recent years is because they want to see external consumption higher than 50 percent. For these companies that have been around forever, the big, critical aspect that people point to is there's no real customer at the end of the day, it's just a bunch of distributors signing up other distributors and it's all internal consumption sales.

With our refer two model, the customer acquisition bonus and the free-to-join concept, we've done something at Le-Vel that has never been seen before. As of 2021, we have more than 1 million promoters in our company and more than 10 million customers. When you look at our internal revenue versus external revenue, and you see how top heavy we are on the customer side of the equation versus the promoter, it's extremely rare in our industry. Those numbers are a completely inverted model unto the stereotypical company. The best I've seen in the industry is close to 50/50 customers to promoters revenue, and Le-Vel is somewhere near 80/20. And while our customer base has been revolutionary, our retention is higher than the industry standard. Not only are we retaining people longer, our "wallet share" actually grows, meaning every time users hit our shopping cart and place an order, it gets larger and larger and larger. That speaks one billion percent to the efficacy and quality of the product and the belief in our product-driven culture. There are some great companies out there in the direct sales industry but what Le-Vel has done in our customer revenue versus promoter revenue are numbers that are extremely rare in this space.

The deeper you dig and the further you look inside Le-Vel's engine, the more you will uncover how this company is different. It's evident in how we operate but also in our compensation plan, how we pay, our incentive trips, our culture, our trainings, our product line.

Everywhere you look, Le-Vel strives to be different. Le-Vel *is* different.

CHAPTER 16

What Makes a Successful Company

Tracy and I had just started dating when one of my best friends at the time, Drew, invited us to his lake house about an hour outside of Nashville. I was dead broke, trying to find my way in the industry, and Drew was a successful dermatologist who seemed to have everything figured out. Yet I still had this bravado that, while it might have seemed misplaced, it was part of both my mind and my conversations. After a long day of water skiing, Tracy and I sat alone in the hot tub listening to music and staring at the stars.

"I'm gonna be successful," I told her. "I promise."

There was nothing that pointed to this vision being true, but it was a feeling that I had for my life. I wasn't being egotistical when I said it, but I knew what it took to become successful. It was almost like, "Put me in coach, I know I can do it." That feeling inside was so immense. But as you've read, my journey was not easy. It's one thing to declare your desire to be successful and another to go through shit to get there. You have to want it. There were times where I certainly felt the opposite, when I was defeated or facing adversity. In those moments, it's not always easy to continue thinking that way. That night, for whatever reason, I was filled with confidence.

I always felt like I was different and that there was something different for me in life. When you're young, you don't really know what that means, and I don't know if I can truly explain it even now. But I remember being in high school and knowing the path for me was not going to be like it was for others. I came from a very humble upbringing, so it wasn't a sense of entitlement. But I felt I had the God-given abilities to achieve something. I'd always felt that. Lubbock, Texas, was full of great people, but they were completely fine paying bills, punching a clock and heading home at 5 p.m. That life scared the crap out of me. I saw good people with no drive. That still scares me today. Some of my friends from that time period are doing the same things that they did years ago.

My advantage wasn't educational. I hardly went to college. I started at South Plains College, moved to Lubbock Christian University and then transferred to Texas Tech University. In total, I spent roughly two years in college before I dropped out and jumped into the business world at AdvoCare. It wasn't like your first job where you just take it slow. Bam! I was thrown into this high-level way of thinking and people that wanted to succeed. As soon as I was shoved into that business space I knew immediately I didn't want the average life. I think my internal wiring to be hyper competitive played a role. I've never thought in terms of having to outdo someone. I am driven to succeed. It's how I view myself. People are driven by different things in life. Some people love the win, and other people love the recognition. Some people love to be recognized way more than the win. Leaders like recognition, but babies cry for it. Sure it's nice for people to know I've won or done this or done that, but at the end of the day, if I had to pick, just give me my win and I'll quietly go down the road. Nobody has to know. That's what it was for me. If I am here, I naturally want to go there. I just want wins. Isn't that what all people should aspire to?

At AdvoCare, I started meeting people that thought differently than anyone I had been exposed to in my life. I started meeting people that dreamed like me. I guess that's what took the cloak off the rest of the world. Every night after dinner in Nashville I'd sit in my little bitty apartment, completely broke, researching every company I could think of. It was the dawn of the dot com boom and you could visit these company websites, look at their comp plans and see their product portfolios. I would stay up into the late hours of the night studying all of them. What was I looking for? Success. I was so consumed. I didn't party. I had a social life but only on Saturday nights. I never left the idea of success. I learned what everybody was doing. I earned a self-taught PhD in the direct selling industry. But it also drove my desire. I would see these companies succeeding on a massive scale and it drove me nuts. It was right there in front of me. It could be done. Being a student of the direct selling industry taught me so much, but pursuing it drove my desire up—all the way to Le-Vel. You can take desire and sharpen it and transform that into competitiveness, but I don't think you can teach desire. That's what I call dragging someone across the starting line. You've got to want it.

AFTER DOING $10 MILLION in sales during our first year, Le-Vel had reached $350 million in annual revenue by 2015. I fully realized our success as I sat at my computer at 5:30 a.m. one day when the top email caught my attention. The name of the sender was odd: Lizard Squad. I opened the email and started reading: "Hi Jason. We are the Lizard Squad Group. We are the notorious group that hacked Sony PlayStation …" it read, listing big companies the group had hacked. "This email is to inform you that as of right now we have 100 percent control of your company and your system. If you do not send us 1,500 Bitcoin by midnight we're going to collapse your system." It translated to roughly $2 million, and the threat continued that if we contacted the FBI, the price would triple. I was laughing as I read further and further. "This is pretty ballsy," I thought. Then I tried to go to our website. It wasn't there. I tried to log into our admin account. It had disappeared, too. Everything was down.

Now I was starting to freak out. As the clock approached 6 a.m. I called our Chief Technology Officer, Matt Glover. "Hey, I got this really weird email," I said. "They're saying that we're hacked and we don't have any control of our system." Matt started firing up the team, and the consensus was that we were under a DDoS attack, where hackers use malware on hundreds of thousands of computers across the globe to send insane amounts of volume to your servers to collapse your system. Imagine 500,000 people trying to go to your website at the same time and then sitting there hitting refresh, refresh, refresh, refresh. Even for the biggest systems in the world, there's a volume that they can't take.

We were becoming a big company and were accustomed to doing a product launch, with anywhere from 30,000 to 60,000 people logged in at the same time and trying to buy the same product. And here we were, getting destroyed. As we investigated we saw that most of the volume was coming from countries we didn't even do businesses in. We started putting a DDoS shield up to deny traffic, but it took nearly 48 hours to gain back control of our company. The attack went on for probably six months, and some days they'd break through and screw something up. Even to this day Le-Vel has between 10,000 and 50,000 failed attempts from people trying to log into our server from across the world. We had to spend thousands of man hours, hire special consultants and spend many thousands of dollars to build an incredibly more secure system. We had to blacklist IP addresses and web traffic from countries we didn't do business in.

It was the price, I was learning, for success. By the spring of 2016, Direct Selling News awarded Le-Vel the BRAVO Growth Award, which is given to the fastest growing company in the world. Out of all direct selling companies in the universe, Le-Vel had grown the most. By growing a whopping $250 million in one year.

I consider any growth a win, but as I've said before, the two most important things to me as the CEO of Le-Vel are the safety of the company and innovation. You want to protect the brand that you created and put so much time and effort into and you try to do the right things and be responsible. I'm always trying to keep Le-Vel moving 60 mph on a 70 mph freeway from a safety perspective. At the same time, we've prided ourselves as being the Ferrari in nutraceuticals. That's difficult. You have to be different to make it in business. In this industry, 90 percent of all companies are in nutraceuticals. That's been the product line that's proven to stand the test of time. There are a lot of companies that have come and gone that are technology-based, but in the nutraceutical space you'll find a lot of me-too products. They all have the same type of product, often just branded differently.

Along my steppingstones, what I saw is the companies that really did well were the companies that had a really strong culture that was emotionally driven and could bring the 'it' factor. Any company can produce a product line, but when you see companies that can really deliver that 'it' factor in the marketplace, they go to the next level. I remember watching MonaVie go from zero to hyper growth, and it was one of the most beautiful things I had ever watched. They checked every box, they did everything right and they had that 'it' factor. Then they messed it all up, managed the business poorly and became an opportunity-selling multi-level marketing company. It is a true shame for a company in any industry to get that big and then disappear.

Because of what I've experienced, for better or worse, I'm always thinking about worst-case scenarios. I've been through so many. Start this company, it's gone. Be with this company, it's gone. I know what it's like to have nothing. I know what it's like to have to start over again. The feeling is awful. I tell my wife—these are the thoughts that keep me up at night. My worst fear is to become a MonaVie or a ViSalus and be gone overnight. It's not only about me. There are hundreds of thousands of people who are in this company, so many livelihoods at stake with every decision. You've got to ship the product, pay your people and handle support. You've got to do everything perfectly to not screw up that moment. The train is constantly ripping down the tracks and you're trying to keep it moving. There's a saying in our industry that too much growth is not good and no growth is not good either. If you're lucky enough, you get to find that balance. Most companies never have the problem of growing too quickly. At all my stops before Le-Vel, I never had to worry about growing too quickly. But if you have the right scenario, like what Le-Vel went through, it took every ounce of everything Paul, myself, our vendors and everyone involved had. I'm not trying to pat ourselves on the back, but when Le-Vel was going from $10 million to $350 million in annual revenue, there's less than 1 percent of people walking this Earth that could successfully navigate a company through that type of hyper growth and not screw it up.

HAVE YOU EVER THOUGHT about everything that has to go right to get a product into a customer's hands? Take Le-Vel's Thrive men's and women's capsules as an example. You've got two capsules in a packet and 30 packets in a box. First, you manufacture the capsules. Once that's done, some companies would slam them into a bottle and ship it off. That's not as premium as I wanted things. So once the capsules are produced you have to set up a packaging machine, which drops two capsules into a packet and seals it. Someone at the end of that line puts 30 packets into a box, seals it and it gets shipped to a warehouse. There are all these moving pieces and components. There's raw goods for the capsules, film for the packet, carton for the box. It's really the supply chain. If we had a digital product and had 10 million people a day that bought that product, we'd have no problem with scale. A zillion people a day could buy that product. When you're dealing with a tangible supply chain and products that need to be manufactured, too much growth can cause a bottleneck. You can't put capsules to packets to boxes to cases faster than the growth is happening. If not done right, that's what can topple you.

I don't know where it came from or how it got there, but there's always been a desire for perfection where I feel little details matter. If you look closely at the environment that we're in today, details really don't matter to a lot of people. That always bothered me. The world today, nobody really cares. They let it slip by, take the path of least resistance. Someone might say, "You're a perfectionist," but that's not what I'm after. When you're a startup like Le-Vel was, people are expecting you to drop the ball, they're waiting for you to prove their skepticism correctly. I knew that because I had seen it again and again, and I wanted to be flawless. I don't care if it's a direct selling company or Five Hour Energy, it's so important to not screw up. I was so military-like about watching every piece of Le-Vel. From manufacturing the products to shipping on time to paying commissions on time to handling customer service. You could tell me my product sucked, you could tell me this, you could tell me that, but you would not be able to say I ran a sloppy operation. That's what I cared about early. We were going to run a tight ship. I was literally doing everything. I was wearing a million hats at once. It became so exhausting in those early days for our three-person team.

I remember venting to my wife one night and waking up the next morning with a plate of folded color sticky notes on the end table. Tracy had put notes on the plate with words like "Customer Service" and "Spreadsheet" and had placed a second, empty plate on her side of the bed as a symbolic gesture for me to take stuff off my plate and put them on hers. She was such a sweetheart. It was an incredible gesture, but the operations of Le-Vel were my responsibility and I needed to handle my plate.

As many companies scale, their operations are toppled. They screw up supply chain, customer service, payment commissions, card processing. Screw any of those up and it's all down hill. In my opinion, if you operate a sloppy company, it speaks to who you are as a person. Are you a man of your word? Are you an honorable person? Are you a company of your word? Are you an honorable company? It all starts from the top down. If someone were to tell me, "Hey, you have a bad company," they're essentially talking to me as a person, who I am. I take it personally. Going through business and having so many failures, for better or worse, grooms you to see moves on the chess board before they happen. It puts you in a proactive strategy mindset on how to prevent those moves instead of allowing the moves to happen, forcing you to react. Where does that come from? Does that come from what happened to Burn Lounge? Does that come from what happened to AdvoCare? Absolutely. It's the greatest concern I have. I've failed forward so many times in my life, but I've learned every time. Because of those misfortunes I can see the landmine that can blow me up. What you go through in life, if you stay at it long enough, shows you how to go through the minefield. All of my failures hurt so badly. The pan was so hot that you never, ever touch it again. You learn from your mistakes.

I learned early on that money would solve problems. Even to this day, I like being able to be known as someone who doesn't owe anybody. When I was handling all of the accounting years back, Friday was my day to pay invoices. Every invoice I got, I paid it. I didn't care if it said 60 days or 90 days. The train was running down the tracks and I wasn't going to try and juggle an invoice for 90 days. Any business is going to have vendors. I don't care if you're a restaurant or a gym, you're going to have vendors that you buy products and services through to facilitate your business model. Even the largest companies in the world have vendors, and vendors will absolutely make you look 10 times bigger and better than you are or they will absolutely break you. Back in the early days of Le-Vel, 90 percent of the challenges we were trying to overcome on a daily basis were always around the product.

What gives you more clout with a vendor than paying bills faster than anybody they have? When you call, they answer. "Jason, what can I do for you?" When we were hitting hyper-growth, and I was having to ask vendors to go buy a piece of equipment or go get a bank loan for $80,000, I would never have been able to ask those things had I not been writing checks every week way before they were due. I knew early on we may not be a big conglomerate, but I could get attention by paying my bills immediately.

Even when the vendors produce, I've spent so much money hiring hotshot drivers. A hotshot is someone that has his or her own truck and beats to their own drum. They pick up their inventory and then they basically don't go to sleep. One of our manufacturing facilities is outside of Los Angeles, and our main shipping facility is in Salt Lake City. I don't know how many times I've had to pay a hotshot to drive overnight and get the shipment there the very next day. If you really looked at the accounting you'd go, "Jason, you're really not making much margin because your profit is getting eaten up by these colossal hotshot fees." But I don't care, because the main thing is to keep things humming. If I make a margin, but I don't ship for three days, it's going to kill the morale in the field, it's going to kill the momentum, it's going to hurt our reputation. From the beginning, I was willing to do anything and everything it took to not screw up. That meant shipping product on time, having inventory to sell, customer service and paying our promoters on time with their commissions.

What's most important is creating that environment to succeed as a team. It's critical to get your people to buy into a team philosophy that we are here to take this to the next level. We have a fiduciary responsibility to the people that count on us. How are we going to compete in one of the most competitive environments that's ever existed in direct sales? Not only that, we're competing against giants like Amazon. We can't screw up. What we do as a team, good or bad, matters. And more importantly, the bad matters. Ironically, people don't remember you for what you did well. They remember you for where you messed up. They don't remember how many times you shipped a product on time, how many times you got things right. They remember that one time you didn't. That's what's so hard in business.

One thing I can passionately say is when I look back at Le-Vel, there's not one ounce of energy, passion or sweat that I've left on the table. I've given my all to this company. We went from zero to $1 billion in sales in less than four years, the fastest company to $1 billion in the history of the industry and likely the fastest to $2 billion. What am I proud about when looking back on those times? I can say I gave it all, literally everything Jason Camper had to give.

As a competitor and as someone who aspires to win, all I want to do is continue to win in all aspects of life. I've often asked my sales force, "Do you want to win?" It's an easy question. We all have to answer it sometime and we all *can* answer it. But does your answer start with a "Why?" My goal is to take my God-given abilities and talents and continue to grow to the next level. Warren Buffett has compounded his money over and over. It's not purely about money for me; I want to continue to win. I want to build wins on top of wins.

Are you the person raising their hand and saying, "Hey, I want to win in life. Help me. What do I do?" You can't pull somebody across the starting line that doesn't want to be pulled.

CHAPTER 17

Dreams Come True

You've seen those underdog movies, right? It's funny to me who those movies move. It's the people who are dreamers and fighters and believers. It's people who can relate to that underdog in the story. I've always loved those movies and have always viewed myself that way. For whatever reason, I've always been this passionate dreamer. But I had no idea how to get there. I didn't come from money, I don't have a formal education, there was nothing given to me other than great parents and God-given abilities that I didn't even know I possessed early on. But I was passionate, curious about what was out there, what I could achieve. I had a great understanding that things in life are not given, they're flat out fought for and earned. If I wanted something, I *had* to make it happen.

I've never been a person to physically write out goals. How I work on a daily basis is I'm very bullet-point oriented about what I need to accomplish. I'm horrible about a calendar. I don't spend a lot of time on that, but I'm constantly jotting down notes and bullet points on my iPhone or papers on my desk. I know what I'm after. I do have a collection of journals from my early days in the industry that I often reference. I have three journals in particular that often come in handy. When I'm plotting my game plan of how I'm going to close a convention or talk to my leaders, I'll sometimes go back to these notebooks and think, "What's something inspiring I can pull from?" Back in 2015, as I was preparing to talk to a room of 500 Thrivers in Grapevine, Texas, something in particular popped in my mind from this one time in Nashville. Over the years there were some times when Tracy and I had moved and I glanced back at the journals, but nothing had ever provided an epiphany. That night I was looking for a good quote, something inspirational to build the presentation around. As I was searching through the journals trying to find the perfect anecdote, I opened one journal and looked inside the front cover.

As I was reading the goals I had written inside, it hit me.

"Holy shit," I thought. "I did this. Every goal I listed here 15 years ago I accomplished!"

I was going through the journals to find something really meaningful that had impacted me early on, and the very journal itself ended up being the impact. I went to the meeting in Grapevine and I told the story for the first time.

I FELL BACKWARDS INTO this industry. Yeah, I was always interested in sports and supplements, but it wasn't until a couple of years into it that I realized how bad I wanted to succeed at AdvoCare and direct sales. I saw it as very obtainable, but I could not get things going in Lubbock. I saw all the stars aligning for Wes. Everything was working for him, he was making all this money and had all these cars. Then there was Danny Mac and Diane, these successful multimillionaires. Yet, there I was, unable to get any wins. I was still dreaming and still believing. Was I crazy?

I was trying so hard to make AdvoCare work, doing everything people were telling me to do. I remember sitting in the car wash at a Lubbock gas station one day when a Bruce Springsteen song came on the radio. For whatever reason I could see these dreams of the future right in front of me. I could feel it and see it, but yet I felt like I was going nowhere. There, in the middle of that gas station car wash, I started bawling. Springsteen's was a feel good song and in that moment it triggered these vivid images in my head of me making it and being successful and getting what I was so passionately after and focused on. Yet, I felt like I was still at first base. It went from this euphoric, vivid dream to, "Man, this is not happening." Knowing what I know now, I would start assessing my situation much differently, breaking it down and really dissecting what was happening and why. Back then, I didn't have a whole lot of knowledge. I didn't have a whole lot of know-how. It was a continual circle. Chasing the dream.

I learned early on that when you talked to Danny Mac you had to be careful because he didn't have any time for negativity and whining. I had seen him cut people off in his life that whined and so I never wanted to come to Danny in a negative way. I wasn't really that type of person. Of course there are bad days, but I don't sit there and whine. I try to get more fired up to go fight a better fight. That's usually how I fix my problems, and back then I was so focused on chasing a dream. I remember going to Danny one time in a really positive way. Danny was very religious. "Jason, the Good Book says, 'Knock and the door will be opened to you. Seek, and you will find.' It doesn't say knock a couple times and if the door is not answered go away or seek for a little bit and if you don't get what you want, then quit," he told me. "Just do it. Just knock. It tells you to knock. It tells you to seek."

That has stuck with me ever since. You may recall from the beginning of my story that I still share that verse with my field to this day. That moment was a realization that I hadn't found the right people, my time hadn't come. It wasn't necessarily that I wasn't pitching the right way. I chose not to dwell on the darkness. It was more about focusing on what was still there in front of me, what was possible. Although it hadn't been possible for me, it was still there and it was still real. There was an insane amount of belief in myself that I could do it. My dad tells me the most painful and frustrating personality trait I ever had growing up is the same one that made me successful. I never took "no" for an answer.

I'm a firm believer that things happen for a reason in life. What I've noticed in life, in business and outside of it, is that things that are supposed to happen have a way of naturally coming together for you whereas things that are not supposed to happen give you pushback and become roadblocks. It's very apparent looking back that AdvoCare was not meant for me, but AdvoCare played a very important part in my life. I always look back at what Danny Mac told me, and I believed it. He didn't know my door would open outside of AdvoCare but it was my commitment to constantly knocking that started the flame and stoked the fire.

I WAS STILL IN my early 20s and had just moved to Nashville when Danny invited me and Wes to his home in Brentwood, Tennessee, just outside of the city. I didn't think much of it. Danny and Diane had moved in from Austin, Texas, and when Danny invited you over you didn't question it. It didn't matter what you were doing, you showed up. There was always something going on in AdvoCare, and Danny had pitched the invitation to his house as a small group training, which wasn't all that unusual.

When Wes and I arrived around 4 p.m., there were a dozen or so people, the majority of whom were all six-figure and million-dollar earners in AdvoCare. All except me. The people in the room had changed their lives with AdvoCare. I had brought a new journal with me. I was really big about these journals back then. I was told, "Your mind will only remember so much, the journal is going to remember everything you put in it. Never leave anything to your memory, always write stuff down." That made a lot of sense to me and I'm a very literal person, so I started carrying a journal. I needed to write things down, come back to them and reflect on them.

Danny's living room quieted as he started off the meeting telling everybody the importance of visualization. He started reading a scripture from Habakkuk. "Write down the revelation and make it plain on tablets so that a herald may run with it." He told us that even in the Book it had taught us to write goals down and get your vision and dreams out there. "I want you to write down anything that comes to mind that you would like to have in life," he said. "What's something that makes you emotional at the thought of getting it in life? I want you to dream. Don't worry about how it's going to happen. Don't worry about how you can get there. Don't be intimidated or not write it down because you don't think it could happen. Just write it down."

I opened up my new journal and started writing. I scribbled a list numbered 1 to 10 on the inside cover. "Big Donzi Powerboat—Any kind I want," I started off. "Buy parents house wherever they want, possibly next door," I wrote midway through the list. "Be able to buy sports cars and various other automobiles," read the eighth goal. Then came No. 10: "Be one of the most successful and wealthiest people ever in direct sales." I closed the journal and didn't think much of the inside cover. Every time I went to a training or a convention I'd fill pages with other goals, notes or thoughts. I was dedicated to learning and hearing from people.

I never really went back to the goals in the years that followed my time at AdvoCare. Back then, when it was slim pickings, it was almost hard to even open those pages. You knew what was written, but your head was down, your tail was tucked, and it was hard to go back and acknowledge it. Then there were goals sprinkled throughout the journals that had an end date. Everybody tells you, "Write your goals down. Write your dreams down." I didn't have to go back. I knew what I put down on the pages that followed. I had missed goals and promises to myself for many years. Missed them by a long shot. That didn't stop me. There are a lot of people that when they miss goals, they find themselves stopping. While I certainly had some sense of defeat, I was not defeated. I lost some battles along the way, but I didn't lose the war.

What was so cool when I rediscovered those 10 goals as I prepared for my meeting in Grapevine, Texas, that night is that every one of those things today has actually come true. That epiphany ended up being the inspirational message I shared with all those Thrivers that night.

It wasn't only the journals. Think about how many people were in AdvoCare at the same time I was who had journals like me. They didn't all go to the next level. It was the perseverance and the willingness to go for it. I tell people today that I have three journals that have led to billions of dollars in sales. That's how I view it. What I learned along the way was absolutely priceless. AdvoCare and my other stops were the foundational steppingstones to groom me in this industry.

By the end of 2016, as Le-Vel neared $450 million in sales that year, I sat down at my desk in Dallas. Le-Vel had seen crazy, colossal jumps of revenue from $10 million in Year 1 to nearly $500 million four years later. We were growing the company and moving so fast that it took everything—every ounce of sweat, passion, knowledge and experience that I had and the team had to keep the train on the tracks. The supply chain, manufacturing, payment commission, regulatory, support. We bootstrapped Le-Vel out of the gate. We weren't heavily funded. It took everything in me. Had I not gone through all those horrible times, all those learning grounds and the steppingstones that prepared me to manage and operate the company, I would have never known how to do it. In the back of my mind, I'm always scared and afraid that it's going to fall apart like everything else has fallen apart on me. We were growing by hundreds of millions of dollars a year, and I never smiled, never hugged my wife. I never stopped and smelled the roses. I was so focused on growing Le-Vel and praying every night for favor and protection, because I was so scared that it was going to vanish.

As I sat alone in my office, I began writing the video script for *Thrive to a Billion*. The script began in 2012 showing Le-Vel's first order and continued through all these memorable moments. When I reached the end, I broke down crying uncontrollably. Suddenly, it hit me. Jason, you did it. You freaking did it! Everything I'd done to get to that moment… and I had never stopped to acknowledge any of it. It was so surreal, like a dream come true. I finally sat back in my chair, took a breath, smiled and cried. I grabbed Tracy. "What's going on?" she asked. "We did it," was all I could say.

She looked at me confused, starting to cry herself. "You're just now seeing it?

"Are you going to smile now?" she asked. I've been smiling ever since.

People ask me all the time, "If you could do it over again, what could you have done differently?" I'm never able to answer. Everything turned out so well. I don't know how it could have been any better or how I could have done things differently. I certainly didn't stop and smell the roses. Maybe I should have. The one thing that I'm the proudest of is that I can look back and I can passionately say I didn't leave anything on the table. I gave Le-Vel every ounce Jason Camper had to offer. And that feels really good. It's weird sometimes how life works when you have a dream and put it out there into the universe and go pursue it.

Dreams do come true to those that keep knocking and keep seeking.

CHAPTER 18

Looking Ahead

When studying winning people and winning attitudes, I've always been fascinated by what makes them tick. Can you teach somebody to want to win? Can you train someone to win in life? Look at Michael Phelps. Did somebody teach him to have the drive to get 23 Olympic gold medals? Did somebody teach Usain Bolt to not only set a world record but then want to beat it? You look at these people across the world who have a high level of *want*. They compete and they win. Then they *want* to go win again. And again. And again. They want to do it better. I don't think you can teach desire. That's where it all starts. Maybe you can teach somebody how to be competitive and how to train, but it's the desire that somebody has to have for their life. You can get out of a seminar and be motivated, but if that's what drives you, then what? Winning in life is about having an internal drive that allows you to be so focused on something, to want something so bad that you break through every barrier; you overcome all adversities to get what you want. That's what I find special about special people.

When I watch Alabama football in the fall I always crack up watching head coach Nick Saban on the sidelines. He's killing it, his team is ahead by 40 points and he's ripping his offensive lineman for not executing a block. He's so livid, and you sit there thinking, "Dude, you're 40 points ahead." But it's that level of drive and execution and care that defines the great ones.

I try to have that mindset operating Le-Vel. We don't screw up. We care about the details. As a competitor, and as someone who aspires to win, that's what I want to do is continue to win in all aspects of life. When I'm on a leadership call with our sales force, that's my message. "Guys, let's go to the next level," I tell them. "Do you want to win?" I always ask myself how I can take my God-given abilities and talents and continue to take it to the next level. It's not solely about money for me. I want to build wins on top of wins. That's what makes the real champions in the world special—they're able to build upon wins and stay focused on getting better. In my personal life I'm lucky to be in a space where making more money doesn't change my lifestyle. Maybe I'm able to make a bigger impact for charities and causes, but it is no longer a driver for me. My drive is sustained excellence. Being able to double what I've done, that is the driving force for me. That's my own personal scoreboard.

When you talk about winning in life and succeeding, you would think that's a natural hope for someone, that they want to achieve a goal and celebrate it, but then keep going. Look at the New England Patriots through all those years. Why wasn't one Super Bowl enough for them? They won, celebrated and then came back the next season saying, "Here's how we do it better." It's that attitude of winning, exceeding and excelling that you either have or you don't have. In business, that's where my head is. What drives me?

It's that question: What's next?

That's probably been the most challenging aspect these last few years. How do you take Le-Vel's database and leadership group and continually try to go win Super Bowls? That's tough. It can be done, but it's challenging when you're leading thousands of people and everybody is on different levels. Some people are happy being where they're at, but for Le-Vel to really move the needle and make the company jump in a big way, we've got to get everybody fired up at the same time. And that's not an easy task when there are more than a million promoters worldwide. It takes all you can bring to get on a call or a stage and inspire everyone to regroup and go to the next level.

I DON'T CARE WHETHER YOU'RE a great C-Level executive or a wonderful mother, anybody good at something in life has a high level of drive. You don't "semi-care" about how your kids grow up. You really *care*. You've got a passion to see their growth and their life play out the way you'd like to see it play out. I have a very deep drive to win. Today, business is my sport and I like to freakin' win. That's what keeps me laying awake in bed at night and what I focus on when I wake up every day. How do I take Le-Vel to the next level? How can we be different? What do we do now? I'm always standing with a marker at the drawing board in my head. Great, we pulled off Derma Fusion Technology, we were the first cloud-based direct selling model, pulled off arguably the most effective nutritional system in the history of supplementation, generated

231

billions of dollars in sales, acquired more than 10 million customers and paid out over a billion dollars in commissions.

That's all great…but yesterday is yesterday. What's next? Nothing is good enough. You're never finished.

I'm not trying to tell you that it's always easy and glamorous or that there won't be losses along the way. You've read my story. I've been at the lowest of lows and had plenty of losses along my journey. It's tough. I never looked back or changed directions. Maybe I thought about it, but I always looked for another steppingstone to take me where I wanted to ultimately go. Stacking wins isn't easy either. Sometimes it would be easier to take the win, sit back and relax. What are you willing to sacrifice to claim your next win? Le-Vel has had plenty of wins, but competition is tough. If we were to let off the gas and enjoy our moment, there would be plenty of nutraceutical companies looking to try and catch up. No matter what you do in life, there are always people or companies waiting for you to let your guard down. Taking Le-Vel further and coming up with the *next big thing* is part of my job. I'm the product guy and the marketing guy, so anything revolving around advertising, promotions or products is on my back. Is there pressure in that? I don't view it that way.

I see innovation two ways. You can always look at what everybody else is doing and get a consensus. Any leader of a company, regardless of the industry, should be a student of the industry and know what the competition is doing and have a feel for the status quo. One side of innovation comes when you look at what the industry is doing and find a way to do it differently and not fall into that status quo. But the innovation that really moves the needle is doing what has never been done before. It's completely out of the box. Let's say we're going to start a pillow company. We could be successful at creating average pillows on a large scale. That would bore me to death. I don't want to settle for the status quo. Instead, I would look at the pillow industry and ask the critical questions:

How's everybody else doing it?

What hasn't been done yet?

What can we do that's out of the box?

You've got this field of brown cows in the pillow industry. Let's be the purple cow. I approach life and business by looking at how everybody else is doing things, and then trying to do it a little—or a lot—differently. That's what I consider being novel. Then, if you're good and put enough time into it, and a little luck comes your way, you can stumble on how to be truly unique.

As we've built Le-Vel, we've always been driven to be novel and unique in everything we do. Since I can remember, all the way back to my days in my tiny apartment, I've studied what other companies are doing. When Paul and I started Le-Vel, we knew all about the industry and the compensation models that ran it. We were willing to build on that and take everything to the next level. We said, "The industry does this, and we want to be better." We were willing to pay more and do it differently. That's what I consider novel. You're willing to go further and you're willing to do things differently. Today, we've got the No. 1, most aggressive, car plan in the industry and we pay the most money on the least amount of sales volume. We did it bigger and better than anybody else. We've combined novel ideas like that with truly unique ones to grow Le-Vel into what it is today.

DFT was our most innovative product. There have been other companies that have come after us with copycat products, but ours was so well engineered that it was impossible to replicate. It's like saying there have been several attempts at a Ferrari, but they resulted in a Honda. Nothing even comes close. Being unique is about looking at trends and what you feel are going to be the next big things on the horizon. Those are hard because they are revolutionary products. Those don't come along very often.

One thing about business is you have to be realistic. You can't find that unique *thing* every month or even every year. By now, you know I like to look at Apple, a company that's had one of the most iconic runs in our lifetime. Apple completely shifted the industry when it brought out the iPod, and then did it again with iTunes. Not only did Apple leverage the trend of the mp3 digital playing device, it took control of the library source. But even they hit a wall. Even the great Steve Jobs had to ask, "Where do we go from here? What do we do next?" He was always seeing the trend, seeing what was next. He's such a great example because at any company, someone has to be so intensely focused on finding the next idea. It has to matter to them at a very high level to be unique, to be different and to determine what's *next*. It's not easy and it can come with pressure but I love being the idea guy. If you're someone who feels you have great ideas and can combine those ideas with determination, hard work and a dedicated mindset, you can be a great entrepreneur, too.

I don't feel it as pressure or a burden, because it's what stimulates me. It's what gives me satisfaction. Going back to my example earlier, I don't want to be the normal pillow company. I want to be the best pillow company. I don't want to do anything normal. How do we do it better? How do we do it differently? Those are questions I ask myself daily. I'm sure there are some expectations from the field for Le-Vel to keep innovating, but I don't focus on that. It's my own challenge that drives me. Jason, what are you doing now? Luckily, in my industry, having a great product line goes back to another football analogy. Not every product has to be a quarterback. It's OK to have a great wide receiver or a good tight end. Not every product is driving the business. I like to call them, "Oh, by the way" products. Those revolutionary products, if you can latch on to the right one, can drive your business to crazy levels. Going back to the Ferrari, you don't have to question if a Ferrari is great or the best. It's assumed. Lucky enough, we've got that culture at Le-Vel. Our field and customers expect that whatever comes out is going to be great.

At the end of the day, it's a pressure I put on myself, not a pressure that I feel from the industry, because I want to win in all aspects of life. That's what I'm fighting for. How can I be unique? I get satisfaction from being unique. Who wants to be status quo? I don't get any stimulation out of that, so if I can truly be unique and do something differently, that's where the real satisfaction is found. I take pride in being able to say we're the first ever to do *it*. A lot of that has to do with how someone is or is not wired, that nothing-is-ever-good-enough attitude to keep the pressure on yourself. I don't think you can teach that to people. You either care and you have that drive to be the best and always be better— or you don't.

Today, you can look at everything Le-Vel has accomplished and it still goes back to that question: How do we do it better? To me, that's the mindset of any winning organization and champion. You win another Super Bowl and it's back to the drawing board, figuring out how you can do it again. Only better. When I stand in front of 20,000 people at a convention, that's my message.

The world has not seen the best of us yet.

CHAPTER 19

Do the Do

So, you want to be successful?

There are hundreds of self-help books and speakers out there that will teach you the technical side of how to manage your time, how to block out your calendar and how to be operationally in sync. That's fine, but when you really look at why people are successful, no one on Earth is successful because they were really good at their calendar. They were good in their heart. That's the horsepower. You have to remember the three D's: Desire, Dedication and Determination. At some point in your life, you have to hit that all-or-nothing mentality to go accomplish whatever you want in life. If you want to be successful, how bad do you want it?

Do you have the mentality that, no matter freakin' what, you're going to go accomplish what you want? I don't care how many times you fail. Keep going. What is your hot button? Maybe you can't stand that your kids go to childcare. Maybe you envision a better life for your family. Maybe you're just sick of the status quo. If you dig deep, there is something that has to power you emotionally. Whatever that is, harness it and use it to drive your desire and your want to go win. Dial it in, fine-tune it and use it as your fuel. You're never going to win in life or succeed at a high level just by managing your calendar. That's all great, but show me one person that knocked the ball out of the park that didn't have heart. (Note to reader: To this day, I'm horrible at managing a calendar.)

But I wanted things really, really bad in my life, and as tough as it got—and stretching to reach some of those steppingstones almost damn near broke me—I was so determined to power through. Whatever your goals are, it doesn't matter what it is, just go do something special.

There are people in this world who really don't know how to get it done, but they're not going to stop until they do. They're so emotionally powered by their goal, their mission, the destination that they become unstoppable. They'll do anything.

I don't care where you're at right now in your life. Who told you to quit dreaming? In this world, people get married, have a baby, get a job, and they just stop dreaming. So many people fall into the rut of life, the copy and paste, next day mentality. They start going through the motions instead of dreaming for the future. Is that you?

Take a moment to think: What are you after?

What are you doing?

Where are you going?

Once you've answered those questions think about this: What are your dreams?

How emotional do they make you?

You know that I'm a car guy. I get it, you might want a car, too. But at the end of the day, if you thought about not getting that car, is it gonna make you cry? Does not having it make you mad? No, probably not. You might be bummed out. Let's get a dream that has more emotional horsepower behind it. Life is going to be tough. Things won't go your way. At the end of the day, you're going to be fine if you didn't get that car, but there are things in life that missing them will hurt. What really tugs at you? That's the question I fought to answer over the years. Sure, I love cars, but I wasn't on a mission just to go get cars. I wanted to create a life for myself, and to be able to give back to my family. I wanted *that* so badly. I wanted to be successful in this industry. I was determined to make it.

You're not me, I get it. But what do you want *that* bad? What are your goals? What are you trying to accomplish in the next year? How about the next five years? It's OK if you don't have an answer now or if you haven't really thought about it. But you need to start thinking about it now. What are you after? What are you doing here?

Someone once told me the road to a 1,000-mile journey begins with one step and continues with one more. What is your next step? You can't look at the top of the mountain. You have to look at the step in front of you. There will be times when you slip and fall. Will you get back up? Will you turn around and do something else? The day you think you know it all is the day you're headed out the door. It doesn't matter how much we know or think we know, we have to be willing to humble ourselves and go back to square one and do it all over again.

You don't have to be at the top of the mountain today or even tomorrow. But do you have the desire, determination and dedication to climb and then keep climbing when you slip? You have to have the desire to get started; No one can pull you across the starting line. You've got to have the initiative. You've got to want this. A lot of people are willing to attend the conference or read the book, but the average person walks out of that room that they spent $1,000 to be in and can't answer: "Why?"

What is your why? Are you willing to live it? It's time to do it, one step in front of the other. Let's take this to the next level.

I'm a guy from little old West Texas with no formal education and no financial resources who had to fight for many years with tears in my eyes while chasing my dreams. If I can do it, you can, too.

Let's freakin' go!

SO THAT'S MY CHALLENGE TO YOU. As for challenging myself, I'm on a mission to double Le-Vel's annual revenue and continue innovating. I now own multiple businesses and have started my Camper Family Office, which does private investing in different opportunities in various industries. I'm super busy, super focused. Who knows what the future holds with all of these new goals and dreams?

Maybe I'll have enough to write a second book!

Afterword

My journey is certainly one of hardship, life lessons and the sheer will to not give up. However, my journey would not have been possible without incredible people in my life.

Let me start with a special thank you to the Lord above for guiding and protecting my path. My life could have gone a million different ways than the one it did, I can only attribute my life's direction to blessings and protection from above.

Thanks also to my ever-loving parents Russell and LaShell Camper who never gave up on me, and to my amazing wife Tracy, who has been a monumental foundation supporting my journey. Love you forever babe.

I'm also grateful to my business partner Paul Gravette. We did it my friend, thank you. And neither of us could have succeeded without the entire team at Le-Vel (too many to list) from the early startup days, to hyper-growth to current days. It takes a team to make success happen and there are so many great people on our team, making sure the company is protected, continues to grow and operates effectively.

To all of Le-Vel's vendor relationships, who have dedicated large amounts of time and effort in supporting the Thrive movement that now spans the globe, I appreciate you.

Finally, great appreciation and gratitude to anyone who has been a positive impact on my life.

—Be positive and grateful in all you do

Jason Camper

Acknowledgments

Just like success with anything, it doesn't happen overnight and it doesn't happen without the right people coming together.

Thank you to everyone who interviewed for the book and aided in the storytelling.

A special thanks to Don Yaeger for the dedication and commitment to make this book come to life. Wouldn't have wanted to work with anyone else. As well as his talented team, including Alex Halsted and Bob Ferrante, for continually keeping the train on the tracks.

And thanks, too, to the team at Envision Books. First class all the way.